Hollywood Legends ir

By James Ford

Hollywoods Legends in Southport

James Ford

2009

Second Edition

Firestormpublishing.com

Copyright © 2009 James Ford

ISBN 978-0-9564635-0-0

Contents

Introduction 1

Acknowledgements...2

Fred Astaire 3

Robert Donat..12

Clark Gable 26

Mae West..35

Judy Garland 38

Laurel and Hardy 46

Julie Andrews 51

Frank Sinatra 55

Peter Sellers..71

A possible visit from Charlie Chaplin 76

Anthony Quayle..79

Miranda Richardson...81

Films shot in Southport 86

Author's note 141

Introduction

Welcome to <u>Hollywood Legends in Southport.</u>

Dubbed 'Paris of the North' - Southport, is a small coastal resort, in the North West of England. Its famous shopping boulevard, Lord Street, is said to have captivated a visiting Napoleon III so much, he used it as a blueprint for the redevelopment of modern Paris.

It is located north of Liverpool and south of Blackpool. It has miles of sandy beach overlooking the Irish Sea. It is noted for a world famous golf course Royal Birkdale and was home to Red Rum, the greatest Grand National racehorse ever.

Beautiful though it is, you wouldn't expect it to be a magnet for Hollywood film stars. It's a quiet commuter / retirement town. Why would film stars come here?

As you will see, several Hollywood movie stars did indeed come to Southport.

This book details their respective visits and gives an insight into their lives at the time. The book also lists every film shot in Southport.

Acknowledgements

Wherever possible I have tried to contact copyright holders and give acknowledgements where appropriate.

Many thanks to:

Matthew Tinker (*Robert Donat article) and **Colette Newman** at Southport Library for their expertise and unwavering support.

Trinity Mirror plc and **Colin Hunt** for allowing their newspaper articles to be reproduced.

Maps of Southport (1909, 1928 and 1955) - Reproduced with kind permission of the **Ordnance Survey.**

David Bushell of **Brown Turner Ross** for legal advice.

Martyn Coleman – IT Guru.

Ann – Editor and motivator.

Fred Astaire

FRED ASTAIRE

Full Name : Frederick Austerlitz
Date & Place of Birth : May 10th 1899 - Omaha, Nebraska USA
Year of visit : 1926 /1927   Age : 27

Background to visit :

Fred Astaire didn't start out as a solo star. He was originally part of a dancing double-act with his older sister, Adele Astaire.
The act was known as "The Astaires."
They both regularly performed dances from the age of five.
Gradually progressing from vaudeville, (the UK's equivalent of Variety shows) to Broadway productions and performing abroad.
You would have thought that Fred was the star act but you'd be wrong. It was Adele who was considered the more talented, by engaging the audience with a running commentary and jokes while they danced. Fred would just smile, keep quiet and dance magnificently.
After many years of travelling, total dedication to their art and thousands of performances, the siblings eventually parted ways.
In 1932, Adele had had enough of relentlessly dancing and performing. Through her stage work in England, she was often introduced to very important people.
The Astaires were introduced to English royalty and it was through these regal connections that Adele, met, fell in love with and married Lord Cavendish, the second son of the 9th Duke of Devonshire. This marital event effectively ended the sibling's professional partnership. There would no more 'double-act'. The newly-weds then took up residence in the picturesque Lismore Castle in the south east of Ireland.

Fred Astaire, now on his own, decided to try his luck in Hollywood.

He did a 'screen test' to demonstrate his dancing, singing and acting skills. Depending on who you believe, the studio executive who reviewed Astaire's screen test allegedly noted, "Can't act. Can't sing. Balding. Can dance a little."

Despite this lukewarm review, Astaire enjoyed a meteoric rise to become possibly the one of the greatest dancers of all time. During his Hollywood career he made over 49 films between 1933 and 1981. In 1950, Astaire deservedly received an Academy award for his services to film musicals. Astaire had a hypnotizing dancing talent. Fans fixation produced some strange paraphernalia, such as LP vinyl records with sounds of him tap-dancing. Now that's entertainment.

Known to his dance partners as a perfectionist, he would practice for hours and hours every day. He was obsessed with getting dancing sequences exact to the point of exasperating his colleagues. This unwavering preoccupation would make the dancing moves that Astaire made, look effortless and easy.

His success was not only due to his remarkable dancing talent, it was also because at that point in time, dancing was an extremely popular pastime. You have to remember that Astaire was popular at a time when there were no televisions, DVDs, computers, game consoles. Dancing was an entertainment that not only took away boredom, but a means to socializing, learning the latest dances and meeting the opposite sex.

What an absolute delight it must have been to have had the opportunity to watch the Fred and Adele dance at the Palais.

The places they visited in Southport : **Palais De Danse now site of Woolworths, Lord Street.**

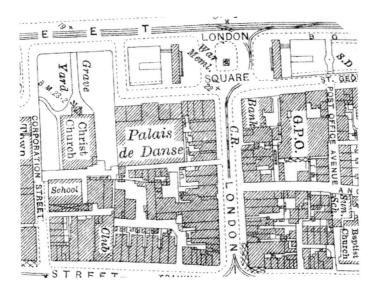

An Ordnance Survey map of the Palais de Danse in 1928.
Lord Street is at the top of the picture and Chapel Street at the bottom.

External shot of the Palais de Danse

A rare internal shot of the Palais de Danse. The stage is to the right of the picture.

Southport Visiter 14th May 1982

Palais de Danse

Report by Cedric Greenwood

It wasn't there in 1924. It wasn't there again in 1930. But for four

glorious years in between, from 1925 to 1929, the Palais de

Danse made Southport the dancing mecca of the North-west.

Billy Cotton's was the first resident band and the Palais was his

first step to fame. Fred Astaire was one of the many famous

dancers who gave shows there.

The ballroom was magnificent and the 10,000 sq ft. parquet floor

was laid on 1,000 springs. It was the largest dance floor in the

North-west in its time.

The Palais was eclipsed by the opening of two ballrooms in

Liverpool – the Rialto in 1927 and the Grafton in 1928. The

opening of the Rialto – which also took Billy Cotton's band from

the Palais – began its decline.

The Palais prematurely ended in scandal and in 1929 the building was converted to the Trocadero Cinema.

The grand, classical edifice was demolished for the Lord Street extension of Woolworth's, opened in 1963.

For a place that occupied such a short span in our time, it left indelible, happy memories in the minds of many local residents.

The Palais de Danse was designed by Southport architect George Tonge for the Southport Amusements Ltd, and opened on May 29th, 1925. (The famous Royal Birkdale Art-Deco Golf Club house is another of his grand designs.)

Other contributions to the story of the Palais de Danse are as follows.

Joyce Poulton, of 45 Victoria Court, Birkdale, recalls : "Saturday mornings, when for 3d, one could sit on the balcony, be served with a good hot cup of coffee and a cigarette and listen to Mendel, the blind pianist play some favourite tunes."

Her letter goes on : "The entrances were opposite the bandstand, where the late Billy Cotton and his band played for the evening dances.

"To the left of the bandstand, looking at your picture, sat the male and female partners, the men in elegant tail suits and the ladies in evening dress. On payment of 6d, one could select a partner for a dance.

"I enjoyed watching the expressions on the faces of some of the partners, especially the males when ladies of my age group now paid more than 6d to dance.

Mrs. Annie Cooke, of 32 Quarry Road, Thornton, writes: "Seeing the picture of the Palais de Danse brought back memories to me. It was there that I met my husband 54 years ago.

"I remember seeing Fred Astaire and Adele Astaire in an exhibition dance and Billy Cotton and his band.

Our final contributor to the Palais de Danse story is the man who sent us the evocative photograph of the ballroom and the photograph of the façade with the Frank Ford banner. He was a gigolo, one of the professional dancers at the Palais in 1926 and he prefers to remain anonymous.

He said: "It was a beautiful place to look at from the outside and the inside. What's there now is an eyesore.

"I believe it was closed down because a few of the councillors got annoyed about a scandal involving their wives and some of the professional dancers."

Mrs Nora Schofield, 90 Rufford Road, Crossens recalled, "There was a sensational court case over the Palais. One of the waitresses was accused of stealing cutlery, which she said she was borrowing for her niece's wedding. She made insinuations about things going on in the rooms off the balcony. After that the Palais was closed."

Robert Donat

Full Name : Friedrich Robert Donath
Date & Place of Birth : 18th March, 1905 – Manchester, England
Year of visit : 1936   Age : 30

Background to visit :

Robert Donat was an Academy Award winning, British actor. He famously played the hero in Alfred Hitchcock's film, "The 39 Steps,"(1935).

Five years later in 1940, he beat off the challenge from Clark Gable to pick up the Oscar for Best Actor for his portrayal of teacher, Mr. Chipping in the film, "Goodbye Mr. Chips"(1939). When you consider that Gone With The Wind virtually swept the board for Oscars in 1940 (It won a record-breaking 10!) for someone to win an Oscar in another film meant they had to have a rare acting talent.

Donat was indeed extremely talented, but life was far from easy for the star. He had a speech impediment as a child, which he gallantly overcame and he also suffered from chronic asthma. It was a respiratory disorder that would prematurely claim his life at the relatively young age of 53.

When he came to Southport in 1936, Donat was extremely well-known because of his roles in the "39 Steps (1935)" and "The Private Life of Henry VIII (1933)."

Donat had turned down roles in Hollywood in order to showcase a play called Red Night (This was developed from a WWI novel by James Lansdale Hodson called 'Red Night – Grey Dawn'. He decided he would premiere Red Night in Southport. Donat had a huge affection for the stage.

It was a love affair which had started at the age of 16 and was 'temporarily disrupted' at 27 when he began acting in films.

For such a famous film star to premiere a play outside of London was very rare, although The Garrick was a state of the art theatre at the time, and was easily capable of meeting any production company needs. Maybe performing outside of the capital would be cheaper, out of the gaze of London's caustic theatre critics and it would have a more appreciative, tolerant audience.

Red Night proved to be a huge hit. When Donat came to Southport, he brought with him a little-known actor called John Mills.

John Mills, went on to become an Oscar-winning star in his own right, for his performance in Ryan's Daughter(1970). He was awarded a knighthood in 1976. He starred in over 120 films. One of which was the classic film Ice Cold in Alex also starring Southport-born, Anthony Quayle.

In an interesting aside, there were rumours that Robert Donat had ordered a house to be built in Hillside. As well the newspaper coverage of the play below, there is the letter from Mr. Donat, dealing with the house he was purported to have had constructed.

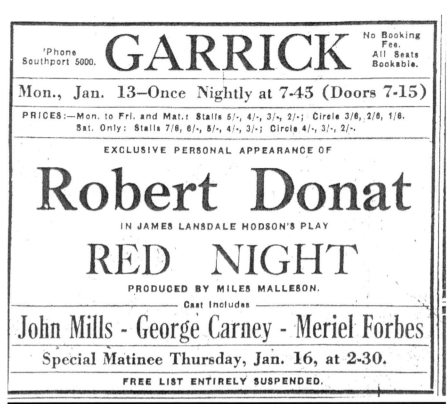

This is the actual advert for the play.

Newspaper coverage :-

Southport Visiter 14th January 1936

BRILLIANT PREMIERE AT THE GARRICK
RED NIGHT
A GRIPPING WAR PLAY
Mr. Robert Donat as Actor-Manager

What promises to be a very successful career of actor-

management was embarked upon by Mr. Robert Donat at the

Garrick Theatre last night, when he presented Mr. James Lansdale Hodson's gripping play, "Red Night," in a manner that deeply moved and won the hearty appreciation of a crowded audience. Fine work was done by every member of the excellently-chosen company, and the applause carried a conviction that augurs well for the future of the enterprise which will go to London after a brief provincial tour.

The author was in the theatre, but he did not respond to the customary calls.

There were numerous "curtains" at the close, and Mr. Donat acknowledged the enthusiastic reception. "It would be indeed ungrateful of me," he said, "if I did not say how proud I am, as a Lancashire man, to have presented this play by a Lancashire author in a very beautiful Lancashire theatre to the most perfect Lancashire audience in the world. My only regret is that our producer (Mr. Miles Malleson) had not the foresight to be born in Lancashire too, because anybody who knows anything about the theatre will agree with me that we, the author and the company owe to him a very deep debt of gratitude."

The premiere of the play was certainly a brilliant one and nothing was lacking in the way of first-night atmosphere. The theatre was filled to capacity, and the representative audience included the Mayor and Mayoress (Councillor and Mrs. T. Ball), who occupied a stage box.

In the days of the old Opera Hose, Southport was often selected as the touchstone for new plays, and it will be recalled that among the big successes that made their debut here were "Tons of Money," "The Sport of Kings," and "On Approval."

The Garrick Theatre, however, has only seen the start of one such venture, prior to this week, this being "The Iron Duke," which was produced by Mr. Matheson Lang, and which, though in many ways a worthwhile play, was not heard a great deal about afterwards.

But "Red Night" will, we believe, have a much happier fate, not alone because Mr. Robert Donat is at the helm. It is true that he enjoys a popularity sufficient in itself to draw the crowds, but the play has merit enough of its own to make it well worth seeing.

In a prologue and three acts, the play is adapted from Mr. Hodgson's novel "Grey Dawn – Red Night," which was one of the successes of its year, and it reveals, in both dramatic and entertaining fashion, the horrors and humours of war. It is the work of a journalist, one who has been at the nerve-centres of national newspapers, and who knows the value of crisply-told incident and the quick interchange of comedy and tragedy. No need to say that he himself served in the war. Only one who actually went to the Front and personally experienced such scenes as are portrayed in "Red Night" could set them down so vividly, so realistically, so naturally. One can vouch for the truth of all of them.

But after seeing the play, one may well ask "Cui bono?" Is there any useful purpose in a war play or a play about war? Possibly to many of the young people of today, the stark horrors of the last war, the war that was to end war, are unrealisable. "Red Night" leaves nothing to the imagination. It shows you what war really is, shorn of its glory and its sentiment. It shows you how fine fellows went out bravely, cheerfully, eager to get to grips with the enemy, and it shows you how the ranks were steadily and relentlessly diminished, how they gradually lost that flush of gallant patriotism, and became puzzled pawns in a game that never seemed to have an end until the bullet or shell brought it. But above all, perhaps, it seeks to show the futility of war. As Private Hardcastle says, "It seems so damn silly?" And it isn't!

Mr. Hodson has made his chief character of Private John Hardcastle, a journalist who joined Kitchener's Army and went to the Front in November, 1915, after taking a fond, hopeful farewell of his bride. And journalist Hardcastle remains to the end, though he tries hard enough to be a soldier and to do his duty. To such men as Hardcastle, the war was hell. Their horizon was not bounded by the trench parapet. They saw the combatants on both sides as individuals, as human beings, not puppets; their creative instinct revolted at senseless destruction. They cried out against the apparently fatuous orders of headquarters; they were irked by the essential routine. And in the play we see how Hardcastle loses his grip, though desperately fighting to retain it. Most authors fail in their last act, but Mr. Hodson achieves his triumph with it – a triumph of tragic drama and the irony of fate. In a battered front-line trench before Le Transloy, Hardcastle and his few remaining pals have been for three days without food, and he is reduced to such a state that is about to inflict a wound upon himself to get a "ticket for Blighty."

As he is about to pull the trigger, his officer friend rushes into the trench, and so Hardcastle is saved disgrace. And then comes the news from headquarters that he has been given his long-awaited commission. He leaves the trench, but returns for his rifle by the parapet...and meets his death.

At last the end has come for him with the dawn.

The play is wonderfully produced and we would join Mr. Donat in offering congratulations to Mr. Malleson. You see here trenches just as they were, with all their cluttering paraphernalia, dimly-lit dugouts, crude estaminets which were palatial hotels to the war-wearied men. Authenticity is stamped all over the settings, and the series of vignettes which compose the play are perfectly presented.

There is an eloquent atmosphere about all of them, and the bursting of shells and whizz-bangs and the whine of bullets leave nothing to the imagination. In fact, there were times last night, when the very theatre shook.

Private Hardcastle is introduced among a diversified company – Private Ronald Whitman, who afterwards became a lieutenant, sustained by the public school tradition, the man who saw that a job had to be done and set about doing it without asking the why or wherefore; Corporal Ian Haslam, romanticist, idealist, and sentimental, but a gallant soldier; Private Syd Summers, the chirpy Cockney, always ready with a witty jest and who regarded history in the terms of football, especially when it came to clashes with the Scots; Private Harry Hollinwood, the fatalistic Lancastrian, who believed that if you were meant to get one you would and it was no use worrying; and Private Robert McTaggart, the canny Scot, who proudly spoke of the clan of the "kilties."

Mr. Hodson has drawn the characters with unerring touches, and he gives free play to their qualities, especially their humour. Some of the scenes are vastly amusing, not least being the one in the dugout where the men are ridding themselves of unwanted companions!

The play, as has been said, centres round Private Hardcastle, and Mr. Donat portrays this role with insight, sensitiveness, and virility, and yet he does not make it too dominant, for Hardcastle was not one to dominate, though he could do his share at grousing. Mr. Donat, in his well-considered performance, makes us realise very keenly the sense of futility of it, all under which Hardcastle laboured, the gradual deterioration of his morale, and he handles the emotional outbursts very finely, especially the feenzy which is induced by the climax to a series a nerve-shattering incidents. Here is a part which gives Mr. Donat scope for all the qualities which have made him such a notable figure on the stage and screen today, and for the way in which he develops it and blends it into the fabric of the play, we wish him all success in his new venture.

He has surrounded himself with an admirable company, among whom Mr. John Mills, as Private Summers, is outstanding.

Mr. Mills had a big share in the applause last night, and thoroughly earned it. He gives a delightful study of the irrepressible Cockney, as chirpy as a sparrow, and throws off repartee with capital slickness. There is nothing better in the play than his dictation of the letter in which he replies to the impeachments of his jealous wife. Perhaps some of the comedy of this Cockney may smack of the music hall, but Mr. Mills touches it with such typical perkiness that it seems quite natural. Diverting humour is also contributed by Mr. George Carney, as Private Harry Hollinwood, and Mr. James Gibson, as Private Robin McTaggart, whose characterisations are completely convincing, and Mr. Bernard Lee is excellent as the loyal, understanding chum, Private Roland Whitman.

All the other men give their parts full value, and their sincere, spontaneous work, greatly assists the force of the scenes. Miss Merial Forbes, as Stalla Hardcastle, brings poignancy to the parting scene with her adored husband, and Miss Yvonne Andre brings restrained emotionalism to her portrayal of Yvette, the estaminet keeper.

The full list of characters are as follows :

Private John Hardcastle	-	Robert Donat
Stella Hardcastle	-	Meriel Forbes
Private Robert McTaggart	-	James Gibson
Private / Lieutenant Ronand Whitman	-	Bernard Lee
A Pioneer	-	Fred Royal
Captain Wilson	-	Vernan Kelso
Corporal Ian Haslam	-	Guy Spaull
Private Syd Summers	-	John Mills

Private Charles Morton	-	David Markham
Private Thorndike	-	Alick Hayes
Private Harry Hollinwood	-	George Carney
A Private in the Kings	-	James Cumberland
Sergeant Winstanley	-	James Page
A Stretcher Bearer	-	Joseph Scott
A Stretcher Bearer	-	Harry Douglas
A Private	-	Gerald Vane
Clare	-	Helene Lara
Yvette	-	Yvonne Andre
The Orderly Corporal	-	Jack Finlayson
A Drunken Soldier	-	Michael Rae
A Wounded Soldier	-	Dennis Glenny
A Runner	-	Antony Verney

THE ESTAMINET SCENE from "RED NIGHT."

JOHN MILLS, the young film star who portrays the irrepressible Cockney, gives Robert Donat and George Carney, the Lancashire comedian, a light while waiting to go on at the dress rehearsal on Sunday.

Left : MR. ROBERT DONAT photographed in his dressing-room while making-up for the show

Right : MISS MERIEL FORBES, the leading lady in "Red Night," in an informal snap with Mr. Robert Donat.

This is a picture of Robert Donat in his dressing room and on stage at the Garrick Theatre

REHEARSING AT 2 A.M.
ENSURING SUCCESS OF "RED NIGHT"
ROBERT DONAT WITHOUT HIS MOUSTACHE

It was obvious at the dress rehearsal on Sunday that nothing in Robert Donat's show, which opened so successfully at the Garrick yesterday, was being left to chance.

The rehearsal was timed to commence at about six o'clock, but actually it commenced several hours later.

In the first place the lighting had to be just so – every set in the show, there are six, had to be staged and tested for lighting, and then struck.

When the producer is Miles Mallison, this is no rapid task, for not one shadow or glimmer of light out of place on the set seemed to escape his eagle eyes.

During these preparations, some of the players made their appearance, Meriel Forbes, the leading lady, waiting more or less patiently in the stalls for her long-delayed call.

When at last Robert Donat did appear, he was surrounded at once by cameramen and Press, some of whom gasped, for Robert's moustache was gone.

Mr. Donat was more than obliging to the cameramen, he was enthusiastic. He sat on the foyer stairs, slid down the stair-rail with John Mills and George Carney, and even allowed himself to be lathered and shaved with a murderous razor by that expressive Lancashire man, Carney, all for the Press photographers.

The rehearsal, which began at about 10.30pm, went off very smoothly. The play was brought to its thrilling conclusion – this at about 2 a.m – and even then they were not finished. "Just hold that scene for one more photograph," said producer Mallison, and the players posed without a murmur. It's all in the game to them.

Did Robert Donat build a house in Southport?

Here is a letter from the Southport Visiter, 4 years after Donat had performed at Southport.

Southport Visiter 27th January 1940

Robert Donat writes to the Visiter

The Visiter has received a letter from Robert Donat, the famous stage and film star, this week, who says he is trying to unravel the mystery of a house at Hillside, which rumour says he is supposed to have built.

"To my great surprise and delight," he writes, "it has been brought to my notice that there is a house at Hillside by the golf links which I am supposed to have built."

He first heard of it from some Birkdale friends when he presented "Red Night" at the Garrick Theatre in 1936, but an interesting letter in his fan mail brings it once again to his notice he adds.

"I know nothing whatever about it personally, but apart from the fact that I should be most amused to find out how the legend arose, I am beginning to wonder whether I have not been leading a double existence, I fail to see why I should choose Southport, which is about 160 miles from my country home as the crow flies."

The house Mr. Donat refers to is probably that where Mr. John Bowes, the local artist and musician resides. The public have frequently confused his name with that of John Boles, the film star, but Robert Donat is a new imagination of the public.

Clark Gable

CLARK GABLE   METRO-GOLDWYN-MAYER PICTURES

Full Name : Clark Gable
Date & Place of Birth : 1st February 1901 – Cadiz, Ohio USA
Year of visit : 1943   Age : 42

Background to visit:

America entered the Second World War in December 1941 following the attack by the Japanese on Pearl Harbour, Hawaii. To raise money to pay for the cost of the Second World War, the American government sold war bonds. The general public would buy these bonds and get their money back when the war was over.

Metro Goldwyn Mayer, on behalf of the American government, asked Clark Gable and his wife, Carole Lombard if they would go on tour to Indiana and encourage people to buy war bonds. Gable was unfortunately occupied by filming, so Lombard gallantly carried on regardless, accompanied by her mother.

She toured the state of Indiana, raising millions of dollars for the war effort. It was gruelling work that involved long working hours and much travelling.

When the war bond tour in Indiana had finished, Lombard understandably wanted to get home as soon as possible. Rather than take the train home, she decided to travel back to California the fastest way possible, by plane.

Gable was aware of when his beloved wife was coming home, so he spent a lot of time and money getting the house ready for a welcome home celebration.

To Gable, Lombard was the perfect wife. Yes, she was young, beautiful and energetic, but she understood the movie business.

She was an excellent actress in her own right, having been nominated for an Oscar in 1937 for her role in My Man Godfrey (1936). She could be prim and proper but she also smoked and drank. She could tell jokes and wasn't upset by swearing. She also used to accompany Gable hunting, camping and fishing. She was the complete companion.

Although they had been seeing each other since the mid-1930s, Gable and Lombard had only been married since March 1939. Stepping on to the plane, Lombard couldn't wait to be home. She told her mother, she was looking forward to seeing 'Pa', her pet name for Gable.

On the morning of January 16, 1942, on the flight back home, Lombard's plane crashed into Table Rock Mountain. There were no survivors. Upon hearing of her tragic and horrific death, Gable immediately left for the crash site.

Half-way up the mountain, friends implored Gable not to go up any further. What would you do in that situation? Thankfully, Gable spared himself the visual agony and went no further. He did stay to take her body back to Los Angeles by train. After the funeral, he completed the ironically-titled film "Somewhere I'll Find You." and then made a life-changing decision.

He decided he would join the 8th Army Airforce and help the Allies overcome Hitler. MGM were extremely unhappy at Gable's decision.

This is a man who made millions for the production company. He was undoubtedly their biggest star.

Here was a screen legend, the King of Hollywood saying he was going to risk his life in the war. The studio cash cow was entering an already blood soaked, slaughterhouse. MGM failed to dissuade Gable from going.

You can understand the motivation behind Gable's decision but the danger he was putting himself in, was immense.

Nevertheless, Gable didn't use his star status to have an easy time of it. He joined as a private and rose through the ranks. During his time in the Eighth Army Airforce, Gable made a documentary film.

The film was called "Combat America."

Combat America was written, narrated and directed by Clark Gable. It was financed, not by Hollywood but by the War Finance Division, Washington.

It was great propaganda and only showed successful missions and how soldiers were looked after if they were injured.

The film did not show the incredible loss of life suffered by American bomber crews. America, against the advice and experience of the RAF, decided to go ahead with daylight bombing missions over occupied Europe, regardless of the human cost.

On the one hand, missions undertaken in daylight allowed a bomb crew to see what it was bombing and therefore achieve greater accuracy and success.

But on the other hand the enemy could easily spot anything in the sky and launch plane and artillery attacks against a comparatively slow bomber.

Statistically, when Americans went on bombing raids in a B-17 bomber, they only had a 1 in 3 chance of coming back from the mission. Imagine standing in front of 3 doors, death would be waiting for you behind two of them. You have more chances of dying than living. After 17 missions out of a total of 35, American bomber crews were allowed R&R (Rest and Recuperation).

During the Second World War, Southport had the biggest Red Cross Rest Home for American servicemen in the whole of the UK. This is because the gigantic Palace Hotel had been requisitioned by the Ministry of Works in 1939 and handed over to the American Red Cross in 1942.

During a week of R&R, a soldier could practically do anything. They didn't have to wear their uniform or do any work. They could go to bed or get up when ever they wanted to. Best of all, the Red Cross organised dances with local girls.

In the summer of 1943, Clark Gable came to Southport and included the Palace Hotel in his documentary. It showed what American soldiers got up to in the town. You can still buy Combat America and see for yourself. Clark Gable narrates the documentary but he is prohibited from mentioning the exact location of the footage.

For Gable, seeing very young men die in combat, put Lombard's death into perspective. Many people suffered abject loss.

Thousands of families never saw loved ones return. Bereavement wasn't something only Gable had to go through.

Clark Gable eventually left the Army in 1943 after flying several bombing missions over Germany. He returned to making films in Hollywood up until his death in 1960.

He was buried with full military honours. Although he was married to Kay Williams at the time, his final resting place was by the side of Carole Lombard.

CAROLE LOMBARD

Clark Gable's wife, actress Carole Lombard

Places visited in Southport : **The Palace Hotel, The Open Air Sea Bathing Lake and Halsall**.

Newspaper coverage:-

None – Total media censorship during World War Two meant that any news or photographs of Allied troop movement or location, were strictly forbidden.

This meant there were no pictures or newspaper articles of Clark Gable's visit to Southport at the time.

The documentary 'Combat America' produced by Gable, shows American servicemen relaxing at the Open Sea Bathing Lake above(Demolished in 1992) and the Palace Hotel below (demolished in 1969).

This is the Palace Hotel transformed into the American Red Cross Service Club during the Second World War.

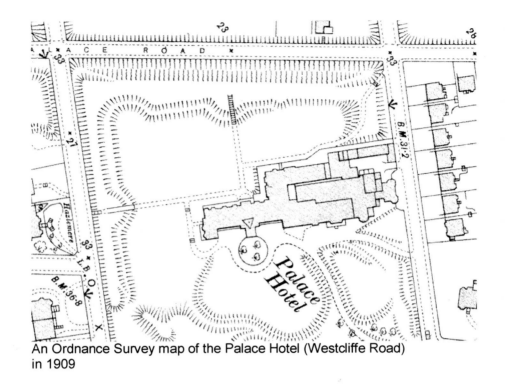

An Ordnance Survey map of the Palace Hotel (Westcliffe Road) in 1909

Here are some letters concerning Clark Gable's visit - obtained through newspaper appeals for information.

I recall an instance when I was 15 or 16 years old, that the Saracen's Head Hotel, Halsall, was visited by the late actor and film star, Clark Gable, who was at the time, staying at the Palace Hotel.

Together with some of his friends, he arrived in an open landau having travelled from Southport, having called at various public houses on the way. They referred to this trip as a 'hayride'.

The party had evidently had a fair amount to drink on the way to the Saracen's Head and once inside, Gable played the piano.

At the time, I, with several others, obtained his autograph.

Mrs. H.Morris, Ormskirk

My husband remarked that he was standing with his friends outside the Scarisbrick pub in Halsall, when three carriages pulled up outside. When who should get out, but Clark Gable. He was very kind and signed many autographs for people. He even did one for the local Bobby (policeman). He was in army uniform.

Mrs. M.Baldwin, Halsall

With regards to the unconfirmed reports that Clark Gable, stayed at the Palace Hotel. This is almost certain as during the war, my late father, Harry, was a Special Constable on duty in the town centre. On arriving home one evening, he said that he had met Clark Gable in Coronation Walk and had a conversation with him, finding him extremely pleasant to talk with.

David.L.Bearton, Southport

Mae West

"A Nice Place, Southport"

MAE WEST with Mr. J. H. Copeland at the Palace Hotel.

Full Name : Mary Jane West
Date & Place of Birth : 17th August 1893 Brooklyn, New York USA
Year of visit : 1947   Age : 54

Reason for coming to Southport : **Invited by Palace Hotel Manager, Carl Muller.**

In 1947, Mae West came to the UK and toured with her own show, Diamond Lil. She had written the play nearly 20 years previously in 1928 and it had remained popular.

Background to visit :

Both an actress and playwright, Mae West is famous for the double-entendre and one-liners. By 1943, she had made 10 films. Tired of film censorship, she believed she had more artistic freedom on the stage than in movies, so she didn't make another film until 1970. Instead she toured towns and cities with her plays. A reclusive personality, it is quite surprising to see her venture out to have dinner at the Palace Hotel.

Yes, she did say, "Is that a pistol in your pocket or are you just glad to see me?"

Places visited in Southport : **The Palace Hotel, Birkdale**

Southport Visiter 4th November 1947

A NICE PLACE, SOUTHPORT

Having heard that Southport is a nice place, Mae West, of film fame, came to see for herself on Sunday, when she paid a flying visit. She was a guest at the dinner of J.H.Copeland, general manager of the Palace Hotel, when others in the party were Kid Lewis, well-known in the boxing world, Mr Myer Castle, Mr and Mrs David Rose and Mr James Timony.

Over in this country with her show, "Diamond Lil," she found time to break away for a little relaxation. From Manchester the play goes on to Glasgow, then Blackpool and later to the Prince of Wales theatre, London.

"Very charming," said those who met Mae West afterwards. She wore a flowing black satin gown trimmed with gold at the neck, a two and half inch wide diamond bracelet glistening on one long black sleeved arm while on one finger she had a 22 caret solitaire diamond ring.

Over her golden hair she wore a dusky pink scarf and she had a dark sable cape.

<u>Judy Garland</u>

JUDY GARLAND   METRO-GOLDWYN MAYER

Full Name : Frances Ethel Gumm
Date & Place of Birth : 10th June 1922 – Grand Rapids, Minnesota USA
Year of visit : 1951   Age : 29

Reason for coming to Southport : **Stayed in Southport while performing at the Empire Theatre in Liverpool**
Places visited in Southport : **The Palace Hotel, Royal Birkdale Golf Club, Southport Fairground and The Belle Vue Hotel, Southport.**

Background to visit :

Judy Garland is probably best remembered for her role as Dorothy in the classic film, Wizard of Oz (1939) although she was twice Oscar-nominated for her roles in A Star Is Born (1954) and Judgment at Nuremberg (1961).

Regarding The Wizard of Oz, MGM studios spent millions of dollars on production. To make sure Judy Garland stayed slim and young looking, she was prescribed drugs to suppress hunger but give her lots of energy and make sure filming stayed on schedule.

Unfortunately, the drugs stopped Garland from sleeping, so she was prescribed sleeping tablets to counter the effects. This is at the age of sixteen.

Judy unfortunately began to depend on the prescription drugs. In later years, as well as chronic drug addiction, she became an alcoholic. Combining alcohol and drugs dangerously increases the effect of both.

In the mid 20th century, there were very few places which could help an individual break their dependency on drink and drugs safely. Judy Garland was therefore, effectively, beyond help.

Too many years of drinking large amounts of alcohol and acute drug addiction would eventually catch up with her.

In 1947, Garland was admitted to a hospital having suffered a mental breakdown brought on by overwork and her addictions.

If an individual gets a reputation as being unreliable or difficult to work with in Hollywood, they might as well forget it. Punctuality and reliability are key to filming schedules. Films are usually made in as quick a time as possible to keep costs down. Being kept waiting by an actor or actress, you still have to pay the director, crew, catering, cameras etc for another day or week etc. Costs quickly mount up.

When Garland stopped turning up on set for three consecutive films, The Barkleys of Broadway (1949), Annie Get Your Gun (1950) and Royal Wedding (1951), MGM sacked her. They'd had enough.

Virtually unemployable in the movie business, deeply depressed and distressed, Judy Garland luckily still had the capability of earning lots of money. This was because Garland had one of greatest vocal talents ever. She could pack theatres just by singing and reminiscing with the audience. Although it seemed like the end to Garland, her fans hadn't forgotten her. In 1951, she toured the UK, to sell-out audiences. In June 1951, she was booked in for one week, to perform at the Liverpool Empire Theatre.

During that week, she stayed at the Palace Hotel in Southport.

After the stage performances, she would often relax and have drinks at the Royal Birkdale Golf Club. Bizarrely, the general public had a chance to meet Garland by going to a dinner at the Belle Vue Hotel on Lord Street West.

Sadly, Garland's life ended in June, 1969, at the grand old age of 47. Her drug overdose was tragically all too predictable.

The journalist who wrote the following newspaper article, must have been ecstatic, when he knew he was going to interview Judy Garland. He probably would have prepared a long list of questions and told family and friends what he was about to do. This is a typical example of how life rarely turns out how you expect.

Newspaper coverage:-

Southport Visiter 19th June 1951

JUDY GARLAND IN SOUTHPORT

The stars and stripes are flying at the Palace Hotel, Birkdale this week, for staying there is famous American screen actress, Judy Garland.

She is appearing at the Empire Theatre, Liverpool, travelling to the city each day from Southport.

Southport Guardian 20th June 1951

HIDEAWAY JUDY SNEAKS OUT TO VISIT FUNFAIR

CYCLONE APPEALS TO HER

Temperamental Judy Garland, yesterday refused all visitors or phone calls and shut herself in her distinguished guests suite at the Birkdale Palace Hotel. But in the afternoon she sneaked out to play on Pleasureland side stalls and take four rides on the roller coaster.

Interviews with the Guardian were twice postponed and then cancelled by the changeable American star. "I don't feel like it," was the only explanation she would make from behind her firmly closed door.

Displaying her 5ft personality in a Liverpool show the brown-eyed brunette from Hollywood arrived back in Birkdale after the opening night at 4 a.m.

She slept till afternoon.

The only phone calls she would accept or make in person are to her five year old daughter Liza, still in the U.S. In Judy's luggage is a set of miniature golf clubs, a surprise gift for the little girl when she comes shortly on holiday. Also destined for Liza maybe the queer little monkey and giant sized doll, her mother won on Southport Pleasureland.

"This is my vacation too," said Garland as she refused hopeful autograph hunters who had spotted her in a rose pink sweater, black slacks and shoes among the fairground crowds. Eager schoolgirl fans who gathered outside the hotel later were shooed away on her 'do not disturb' orders.

Judy avoided the hotel dining room and ate in her suite with secretary Myrtle Tully and manager Sidney Luft. They travelled to and from Liverpool in a £2,500 British 27 h.p. limousine, hired from a London firm.

When she has settled down, Judy hopes to enjoy some of the town's golf links but onlookers will not be encouraged. After her show closes in

Liverpool at the end of the week, she will give a Sunday concert in Blackpool.

On Monday she plans to take part in the London Sid Field Memorial Show. And after that the Garland entourage will move off on holiday - a quiet one.

MISS JUDY GARLAND

This Week

TAKES

AFTER THEATRE

SUPPER

at the

BELLE VUE

HOTEL

DANCING NIGHTLY
(No Extra Charge)

JACK BRILEY and his RUMBA BAND
DINNER, AFTER THEATRE SNACKS
RESTAURANT LICENSED to 11 p.m.

SATURDAY DINNER-DANCE
13 6 incl.

7 30 to 11 45. BOOK YOUR TABLE

MISS JUDY GARLAND
M-G-M. Screen Star
Now appearing at the Empire,
Liverpool

VISIT THE NEW COCKTAIL BAR. **FULLY LICENSED**

Advert for Judy Garland at the Bell Vue Hotel on Lord Street West.

This is an aerial picture of the Belle Vue Hotel.

Here is a postcard of the Belle Vue

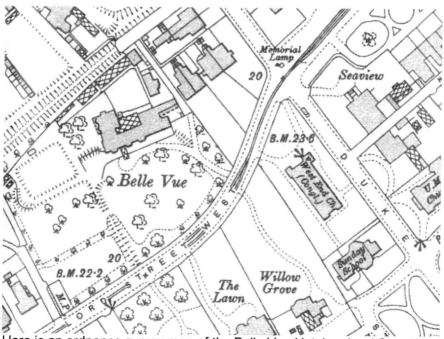

Here is an ordnance survey map of the Belle Vue Hotel on Lord Street West, Southport.

Laurel and Hardy

The wonderful Garrick Theatre on Lord Street. It is one of the finest architectural examples of Art Deco in the North West of England. Designed by local architect, George Tonge.

Full Name : (Stan Laurel) - Arthur Stanley Jefferson
Date & Place of Birth : 16th June 1890 – Ulverston, Cumbria UK

Full Name : (Oliver Hardy) - Norvell Hardy
Date & Place of Birth : 18th January 1892 – Harlem, Georgia USA

Year of visit : 1952   Age of Stan Laurel : 62
                                    Age of Oliver Hardy : 64

Reason for coming to Southport : **To perform at the Garrick Theatre.**

Places visited in Southport : **The Prince of Wales Hotel and The Garrick Theatre.**

Background to visit:

Laurel and Hardy were quite possibly, the greatest screen comedy duo of all time. Innovative, unique and accident-prone, they are undoubtedly the benchmark for all slapstick comedians. Comedies very rarely win Academy Awards (Oscars) but Laurel and Hardy did in 1932 with Music Box. It's a story about two delivery men (Laurel and Hardy) trying to get a piano up a huge flight of stairs on the side of a hill and into a house. If you haven't seen the film or are not familiar with the comedy pairing, this award-winning film is worth tracking down and viewing.

Laurel and Hardy made over 100 films together, between 1926 and 1950.

By the time they came to Southport 1952, their successful film careers were over.

Unfortunately, the much-loved comic duo still had to earn a living, even though they were both in physical decline. Stan Laurel by this time was suffering badly with diabetes. However, this didn't stop them from doing two performances each day.

Five years later, in August 1957, Oliver Hardy would die from a stroke and Stan Laurel would be too ill to attend his funeral.

Newspaper coverage:-

Southport Visiter 19th August 1952

GARRICK THEATRE

LAUREL AND HARDY

Crowds gathered at the stage door of the Garrick Theatre last night to catch a glimpse of Laurel and Hardy, and inside, the theatre was full to capacity.

"Here in person," announced the placards outside. When I was a small boy, if anyone had offered me £100 or the chance of seeing these screen buffoons in person, I would have refused the money.

Accordingly, the small boy in me rose in delight to greet Stan and Oliver when they appeared on the stage. There they were, Oliver of the enormous presence and Stan with his puzzled expression and perplexing habit of scratching his head. Both had those ridiculous bowler hats that have featured in many a rollicking farce. And their amusing signature tune heralded their entrance. As a couple of penniless travellers on a station platform, trying vainly to sleep on a wooden form and getting themselves tied in knots, they had the audience rocking with laughter.

The laughter grew even more uproarious as they blundered about on the stage as housebreakers.

The old tricks and the familiar mannerisms were present and it was truly Laurel and Hardy IN PERSON.

Southport Guardian 20th August 1952

POLICE ESCORT IS ORDERED

LAUREL AND HARDY ARE SCARED OF CROWDS

Laurel and Hardy have asked for a police escort wherever they go because they are scared of being mobbed. Not only police but a doctor and drugs flown specially from the U.S. are keeping this comic pair together on the stage of the Garrick. When they arrived on Sunday they were jostled by a crowd, which led 23st. Ollie to ask for police help whenever he and his slim partner left the stage door.

"We don't want to go anywhere except the back of the stage and our hotel," said Ollie, who saw to it that a 25 horsepower special bodied limousine was at his disposal. The car picked up the comics right outside the stage entrance after Monday night's second house and prevented a throng jamming the narrow alleyway down the side of the theatre from rushing for autographs. In spite of the presence of two policemen, many fans pushed through, simply to touch either comedian's clothes. Some shouted : "I touched him," or "He smiled at me."

Once their 200yd. car ride to the Prince of Wales was over, Stan Laurel went to his room on the first floor and Oliver to his on the second.

Behind the safety of his bedroom door, Stan can relax for doctors have told him he must do nothing else but. His 25 minute turn on the stage is his only exertion.

This morning his doctor will inject drugs specially supplied and give Stan a check up.

Said a friend of Stan last night : "We often wonder how he carries on. He is a very sick man." A special diet has been arranged for Stan, who apparently takes his troubles cheerfully. His big pal, too, has joked about the fact that nowhere can he get a bath big enough for him.

At the hotel special instructions are in force. Neither comic must be disturbed. No phone can be put through until a certain hour. Then, only friends and managers can be connected. Laurel and Hardy, who have made the world laugh for 25 years, turned down Southport Corporation's invitation to judge the English Rose heat this afternoon. Fear of crowds and the extra strain it would put on Stan Laurel were the reasons for the refusal.

THE GARRICK THEATRE

6.20p.m. & 8.30p.m.

ALL THIS WEEK
TWICE NIGHTLY
MATINEE SATURDAY AT 2.30p.m.

HOLLYWOOD'S GREATEST COMEDY COUPLE HERE IN PERSON
STAN LAUREL AND OLIVER HARDY

PRICES 5/- to 2/-
SATURDAY 5/6 to 2/6

Julie Andrews

Full Name : Julia Elizabeth Wells
Date & Place of Birth : 1st October 1935 Walton on Thames, England
Year of visit : 1953   Age : 17

Background to visit :

Julie Andrews started performing to audiences at two years old. As she got older, Andrews went to an arts school where dancing and singing were taken seriously.

Madame Lilian Stiles-Allen honed her protégé's natural singing ability to such a degree, Andrews sang an operatic aria when she was only 12.

When she was 13, she gave a performance at the Royal Command Variety Performance. Her outstanding talent opened doors into both radio and television.

When she came to Southport, the audiences got a seasoned professional. She was not a girl starting out aged 17, but a dedicated, hard-working artist, who had already been performing and practicing for 15 years.

At 19, Julie left England to perform in America on Broadway. Eleven years after her appearance at the Garrick Theatre, in 1964, she would pick up an Oscar for her role in Mary Poppins. In 1966, she would appear in The Sound of Music, and seemingly, on television every Christmas and Bank Holiday since then.

The Sound of Music would go on to displace Clark Gable's Gone With The Wind as the biggest grossing. The current biggest grossing film of all time is Titanic (1997).

Newspaper coverage:-

Southport Visiter 7th July 1953

Julie is a star at 17

She makes her work a hobby

To be a star at 17 years of age is in itself exciting. But learning to drive and wearing a first off-the-shoulder evening dress is proving just as thrilling for Julie Andrews, who is in the laugh, song and dance show, "Cap and Belles" at the Garrick Theatre this week. Daughter of stars, she is a nice, unassuming girl, who loves her home as much, if not more than the stage.

"I go home every weekend to Surrey, to my family," she told the Visiter yesterday.

"I have great fun with my three brothers, all younger than myself, a dog, a cat and a lovely house and garden."

Propped up on her dressing table is a picture of Julie and her father putting in a spot of gardening under the shade of the trees. Work to some people is just work, but to Julie it is fun.

"Music and elocution and lots of dancing, keep me busy most mornings but I love it all. They are my work, but they are also my hobbies," she says.

She does some horse-riding too, but unfortunately has not her riding clothes with her, otherwise she would love to ride on the beach.

Sometimes when she wants to "quieten down" in the theatre before going on stage, she takes up some embroidery.

Now to the thrilling evening gown, which was hanging up in her dressing room. Large silver sequins glisten on layers of tulle shading from blush to rose pink, the off-the-shoulder line outlined with green flowers and becoming to her youthfulness.

Another dress, Which Garrick Theatre audiences are seeing her wear, is old Elizabethan, which she wears for a number when seated on a throne. There are others, of course, but these are the most outstanding.

She started to learn singing at seven years of age and has been on the stage professionally since she was 12. At present she is on a 22-week tour, which will take her to Scotland, Wales and down South.

Since Julie was last in Southport about a year ago, she has done a radio series and had a long season in pantomime with Norman Wisdom.

Tomorrow afternoon she will be seen at the Sea Bathing Lake, when she will be one of the judges in the English Rose contest.

Frank Sinatra

FRANK SINATRA

Full Name : Francis Albert Sinatra
Date & Place of Birth : 12th December 1915 - Hoboken, New
Jersey USA
Year of visit : 1953   Age : 37

Reason for coming to Southport : **Stayed in Southport while performing at the Empire Theatre in Liverpool**

Places visited in Southport : **The Prince of Wales Hotel, Southport, The Palace Hotel, Birkdale and Royal Birkdale Golf Club**

This is an advert that appeared in the Liverpool Echo on Thursday, 28th July 1953

Postcard showing the Prince of Wales Hotel on Lord Street. Early 20th Century picture. Notice the length of telephone number.

This is a postcard of the gigantic Palace Hotel on Weld Road and Westcliffe Road.
On the extreme right of the picture is the Fishermen's' Rest Pub. This is the last remaining part of the hotel. The hotel was demolished in 1969 but the former Palace Hotel vaults were kept open for business.

Background to visit:

Frank Sinatra was an Oscar-winning actor and one of the most popular singers of the 20th century.

When Frank Sinatra launched his career in 1940, he initially enjoyed great success. He performed with big bands, had hit singles, performed concerts to packed out audiences and starred in popular film musicals.

By the late 1940s all this success had gone and his career was nearing the end. Sinatra, did play a part in his own demise. Here's why:

> On April 8, 1947, Sinatra punched a prominent Hollywood journalist called Lee Mortimer at a nightclub. This prompted a lot of negative press coverage linking Sinatra to the Mafia and 'even worse', Communism.
>
> In 1949 he started a much-publicized affair with Ava Gardner, whilst still being married to Nancy Sinatra. This was extremely distasteful to a moralistic, conservative America. The relationship was regularly reported on in many newspapers and magazines which continued for 2 years. To the American people, it appeared that Sinatra didn't care about his wife, kids or family values.
>
> The Metro-Goldwyn-Mayer film production company didn't renew his contract in 1950.
>
> The talent agency (MCA) who had looked after Sinatra, decided to dump him in 1950.

Sinatra divorced Nancy in 1951 against his Catholic beliefs.

In 1952, Sinatra suffered a potentially career-ending vocal chord haemorrhage from 'over-singing'.

Columbia Records dropped Sinatra in 1952.

Had so little money, he was reduced to borrowing it from his new wife, Ava Gardner.

His marriage to Ava Gardner is often described as caustic. The constant roller-coastering between volcanic arguments and equally intense reconciliations made Sinatra suicidal. They split up in 1953 and were finally divorced in 1957.

So you can see, when Sinatra arrived in Southport in 1953, singing on stage was really the only dependable way he could make money. Perhaps it took his mind off all the unpleasant things that had been happening to him. The adulation he received in the UK must have been a refreshing change to his vilified status back home in America.

In Southport and Liverpool, studying the press coverage of the time, his general demeanour is a happy, positive and courteous one although it didn't start off like that.

When Sinatra tried to check in to the Prince of Wales Hotel on Lord Street, Southport, he expected star treatment. Unfortunately, staff didn't recognise him and told him so.

Sinatra, consumed in an apoplectic rage, stormed out of the building and telephoned his friend and golf instructor Bob Halsall, who lived in Hillside, Southport. Halsall advised Sinatra to stay nearby at the Palace Hotel.

Once Sinatra was off the phone, Halsall telephoned the manager of the Palace to warn him of Sinatra's impending arrival. The Palace Hotel welcomed Sinatra and treated him to the sort of respect he was accustomed to.

Before coming to England, Sinatra had made a film called From Here To Eternity. So desperate was Sinatra, to play the part of Maggio, he took a massive pay cut. Also, depending on whom you believe, Sinatra asked either Ava Gardner or Organised Crime bosses to influence the casting director's decision for the part.

During his stay at the Palace, Sinatra realised his run of bad luck was about to change with a telephone call from his management back in America. Sinatra was told that his performance in the film From Here to Eternity, had been well received by film critics. Although Sinatra realised that he was going to get more work in the film industry, he could not have imagined that this minor role would garner him an Academy Award for Best Supporting Actor. This is the beginning of what is often described as the greatest comeback in history. After the Oscar win in 1954, industry doors that had previously been slammed in his face began to re-open. Sinatra signed a new record deal, made many more films and continued to perform to sell-out audiences in America and abroad.

SOUTHPORT GUARDIAN 29th JULY 1953

FRANKIE'S FANS ARE KEPT IN HIGH SUSPENSE

Armed with autograph books, more than 50 teenagers crowded the entrance to the Palace Hotel on Monday morning to catch a glimpse of film star, Frank Sinatra. They were disappointed however, Sinatra could not be disturbed, they were told.

The Hollywood singing star has seen little apart from his private suite at the hotel, since he arrived from Manchester on Sunday afternoon. He was invited to play at Royal Birkdale golf course on Monday but rain deterred him.

He maybe out on the course this afternoon if the weather is fine. Sinatra who is staying at the Palace during this week, topping the bill at Liverpool Empire Theatre, had one sporting diversion over the weekend. Partnered by his manager, he beat bandleaders Billy Ternent and Jimmy Leach at snooker.

SOUTHPORT GUARDIAN 1st AUGUST 1953

FRANK SINATRA PLAYS A ROUND

Free from the clamour of teeming, swooning bobbysoxers, Frank Sinatra enjoyed a quiet game of golf on the Royal Birkdale links yesterday.

Wearing brown slacks and a long sleeved pullover, softly spoken Sinatra took his third lesson from club professional Bobby Halsall. "For the seven months Frank has spent at the game, I have seen no-one pick it up better and I have seen many triers in my time," said Bobby.

The bronzed crooner smiled when the coach added : "If he continues at this rate, he will be giving Bing (Crosby) a game." Idol of millions of cinema-goers, Frank will leave tonight for London and later the U.S., after a spending a week at the Birkdale Palace Hotel, while appearing at the Liverpool Empire Theatre.

Chatting with a "Guardian" man, he said he was charmed with Southport, especially its weather, which had been far kinder to him than at any other time during his British tour. He was interested to know that Danny Kaye had played the same course and said he knew Danny well. The star says he has not been plagued by teenagers here, although he has been sought daily by young autograph hunters. With so vast a repertoire, he cannot decide which is his favourite song and says : "I like quite a few." Before the eager golfer strode off for practice from the 14th tee, with caddy Mr. Thomas (Tich) Rimmer, he was asked to clear up a poser among his fans.

"How do you pronounce your wife's name?" and he replied, "It's easy to remember. Just think of the word 'braver' and then say 'Ava.'"

Then he tried some practice swings in which Crosby and Hope may yet see a challenge.

Bob Halsall was Frank Sinatra's friend and golf instructor

<u>My interview with Bobby Halsall</u>

I became Royal Birkdale's professional golfer in 1936. They paid me a fee.

I was on a basic £10 a week. The fees, I charged for lessons more than doubled my wages. It was then I was introduced to the Palace Hotel by my friends and colleagues.

I had not been at Royal Birkdale very long when I decided to join the T.A. in 1939, to do my bit. I joined with a friend. We just wanted to play at being soldiers. When we went to training we were conscripted into the proper army and told I would no longer be playing golf by the commanding officer. I had to go back to Birkdale and tell them I couldn't play anymore. Birkdale said I was under contract to work for them but I had to join in the war. I was one of the first soldiers to see the horrors of Belsun.

Fortunately when the war was over Birkdale were legally bound to take me back. I'd taught myself everything by trial and error. I practiced a lot to get back to how I was. I was then offered the chance to work at Monte Carlo's golf course and have stayed at Monte Carlo ever since which is over fifty years.

My daughter is there as a professional. The way they have looked after me you wouldn't believe. I keep on reminding them of my age, 'I'm eighty-five y'know,' but they tell me I've got a school to run, lessons to take and your friends are there.

I went to Sacred Heart in Ainsdale. I remember I used to toss a coin to decide whether I went to school or not. Heads I go to school. Tails I go and caddie. And it was caddying most days. I caddied at Birkdale and eventually got an opportunity to be the assistant at Birkdale. I was on 10 bob a week. (10 x 5p)

Royal Birkdale was reconstructed about that time and it was all upside down and so we lost a lot of members. People went elsewhere and I had to go on the dole. I then helped the foreman re-build the Birkdale course. It is a great course and matches any golf course in the world for skill and beauty.

When people came to play I always recommended they stay at the Palace Hotel. We then made an effort to look after the players. We went out of our way to make sure they had everything they wanted and nothing was too much trouble.

Make the visitor feel that Birkdale was 'his own' club I used to say. Don't let him be lost. I knew that without national and international visitors the Golf Club, we wouldn't be there.

It was a crying shame that the Palace Hotel was taken. I don't give a damn whether it was making money or not it should have been preserved and listed for Southport. We're talking about this wonderful hotel, really it was so wonderful.

Karl Muller was my best friend and the manager. Anything we wanted.

I used to play this trick where I'd park at the front of the Palace with some friends and I would ask them to go on ahead because I had to see someone in the Fishermen's' Rest.

I would then run into the Fishermen's' Rest and down the steps, through the cellar and up into the Palace again, and to the bar before my friends had arrived. They used to say, "How was it possible? We left you in the gardens..." and there I was with a glass of beer in my hand. That was my secret passage.

I saw Malcolm Campbell's Bluebird. I met him and he was a gentlemen. He was often there.

The Palace was my hotel and my home. There was always somebody in there that you knew. I always recommended it.

I met Judy Garland there and had tea with her at the Palace Hotel. I played a round with Sid Luft at Royal Birkdale.

I first met Sinatra in Monte Carlo. He didn't play at all. He was with the family of Prince Rainier. When he came to Southport, he wrote to tell me he was coming to tour England. He was not a big name at that time.

I read a book about Sinatra in Monte Carlo by a fellow who hadn't even met him.

How can you do that if you haven't even met the man? You only need to get a man to play eighteen holes to understand him.

Nine holes in fact. A pro can tell what kind of a person someone is by playing a round of golf. How he can take the good from the bad luck and really be genuine.

I decided what time Frank and I would play. He was always on time with me. Frank got a taxi from the Palace and it would be just him and me.

We would play in the morning, he would go to Liverpool in the afternoon and he would say to me that we would have a late dinner together and that he would be back before ten o'clock. And that's how we made it.

Again he was always on time. As a man you didn't feel as though you really got to know him but he was very annoyed when he made me offer I turned down.

"I own a golf course in Las Vegas and I want to come down and be the professional there. Manage the club..." I turned him down because I loved Birkdale and Monte Carlo but sometimes I regret not taking him up on the offer.

When he invited me to his show at the Empire he always gave me front row seats and he used to walk on at the beginning and announce, "I've just had a terrible; wonderful night and there's the man responsible," and point to me.

He was very fit then and he looked after himself during the time he was with me. It's very difficult to do when you spend a lot of your time in casinos and bars.

We both drank whiskey and they were never small ones.

Frank Sinatra would not allow me pay and he always footed the bill.

Every time. Before we started drinking he said, "You've looked after me on the golf course I'll look after you now. I never charged him any fees.

Frank didn't bother going into Southport after he had been insulted at the Prince of Wales Hotel. Frank Sinatra phoned to tell me about the lack of recognition at the Prince. I told him not to worry about that, and that there were other hotels.

I immediately recommended the Palace Hotel and they welcomed him with open arms.

He loved Royal Birkdale and thought it was wonderful. He loved the Palace as well and said it was just like coming home to his own family. Karl Muller, the hotel manager was great fun and knew how to look after V.I.P.s.

We used to go to the top bar overlooking the tennis courts. It was at the end of the week that he received a telephone call that told him that his latest film, 'From Here To Eternity,' had been well received by the critics.

I said to Sinatra, on the night before he was due to leave, that I thought he was a damn good singer with a powerful aura. You stand out I said. Your approach and the way you work with the orchestra and entertain the audience is marvellous. But there are some people who don't think you're that good. Frank asked me whether I believed that and I said I thought he was great.

Frank was furious and wouldn't let it go and kept on asking me whether I thought he wasn't that good.

He then asked me whether I could sing. I said, 'No, I don't sing. I don't know the words.'

"You find something to sing," Sinatra said. "And we'll wake the pianist." Sinatra woke the pianist up and told him that I was going to sing and that we were having a competition. I said to myself, "What am I going to sing?" Frank repeats to the barmaid that we're having a competition and that she is the judge.

There were only four of us, Sinatra, myself, the pianist and the barmaid. If they'd only had video then.

"Do you sing?" Sinatra said.

I remembered a song, "How many times a day..." I used to sing in the bath and thankfully the pianist knew it too. Sinatra sat nearby, looking at me and smoking. So I sang the song as best I could.

"You've sang before..." Sinatra said, taking centre stage.

Frank sang, "Night and Day" and really punished it. We were both drunk. When Frank had finished he immediately asked the barmaid who had won. "Mr Sinatra..." she said.

I said jokingly to the barmaid that I had seen Frank give her a five pound note and she explained that he gave her £5 every time he ordered a round of drinks.

Letters regarding Frank Sinatra's visit to Southport

Letter 1 : With reference to your letter in the Southport Visiter concerning Frank Sinatra at the Palace; no, I am not the barmaid!!

However you may be interested to know that at that time, I was working at Royal Birkdale on vacation from college as a waitress, when Frank Sinatra came to play. We were warned not to ask for autographs or wait to see him as his visits were private.

We did though find out what time he would be coming up the 18th fairway and go on to the balcony of the dining room to see him. I did get a smile all to myself because I was sent out to the bin with rubbish when it was thought Sinatra had gone but he hadn't and was just coming out of Bobby Halsall's shop to get into Bobby Halsall's rather well known open sports car when I was dealing with the rubbish.

So - I got a smile! I distinctly remember his blue eyes and tan and thinking he was taller than I expected.

Yours sincerely

Evelyn Atkins,Southport

Letter 2 :

Dear Sir,

RE - Frank Sinatra at the Palace Hotel

My father, who died some years ago, was Head Waiter at the Palace at that time and he told us a couple of Frank Sinatra stories.

The first related to Sinatra's arrival in the town. was actually booked to stay at the Prince. On his arrival, late in the evening, presumably after his appearance at the Empire, there was a mix up at the check in desk, the receptionist asked for Sinatra's name. "If you don't know my name I'm off," Sinatra retorted and left. Word was sent to the Palace of the incident, the red carpet was rolled out with the realisation that the Palace was the certain alternative to the Prince. Sinatra soon arrived to be warmly greeted.

"Mr Sinatra how nice to see you, we've got the best room in the house waiting for you!"

During that week my father served Sinatra frequently and he was asked whether there was a pub nearby. My Dad took him to the Fishermen's Rest which was then annexed to the Palace and they enjoyed a drink there together.

At that time it is possible that the Fishermen's Rest was run by Duncan Girvan. His main barmaid in the late 50s and possibly the early 50s was a lady by the name of Martha - could this be the lady who witnessed the Sinatra/Halsall song contest.

Time may have played tricks with my memory. I was only 13 at the time but I'm pretty certain with the accounts of Sinatra's time in the town are correct. It would be nice to know the name of the receptionist at the Prince.

Rod Crook, Southport

P.S. My father's name was JOE CROOK.

Peter Sellers

The Garrick Theatre on Lord Street, Southport now Mecca Bingo

Full Name : Richard Henry Sellers
Date & Place of Birth : 8th September 1925 – Southsea, Hampshire UK
Year of visit : 1955   Age : 30

Reason for coming to Southport : **To perform a one-man show at the Garrick Theatre**

Places visited in Southport : **The Palace Hotel, Birkdale and The Garrick Theatre, Southport**

Background to visit:

Peter Sellers was an award-winning impressionist and three times Oscar-nominated actor.

Initially serving in the RAF during the Second World War as part of the ground crew, he went on to become a paid entertainer in the Entertainments National Service Association.

From entertaining the forces, Sellers met up with fellow WW2 war veterans, Spike Milligan, Harry Secombe and Michael Bentine and formed a comedy group called the 'The Goons' in 1950.

The BBC gave them an opportunity to perform on radio in 1951. The Goons unique and surreal brand of comedy was a massive hit with the listeners. So much so, the show lasted for nine further years. By the time Peter Sellers came to Southport in 1955, he was a household name. He had also made a few films but it wasn't until the 1960s that he enthralled a world-wide audience with stellar performances in The Millionairess (1960), The Pink Panther (1963) and Dr. Strangelove (1964).

Blessed with a wonderful sense of comedic timing and an uncanny talent for imitating people, Sellers was box-office gold. It brought him a wonderful lifestyle, house, family, endless sports cars, exotic holidays and many career opportunities.

The fame and glamour didn't make him truly happy. Prone to fits of temper, obsession, vindictiveness, Sellers would often be worryingly unpredictable and petty.

Was it a superstar lifestyle and having lots of money that made him like this or was it an underlying personality trait. As much as he was self-centred, he also had a terrible self-loathing.

Starring in Jim Henson's, The Muppet Show, in 1978, Sellers famously remarked, "There is no me, I do not exist. There used to be a me...but I had it surgically removed."

Newspaper coverage:-

Southport Guardian 10th September 1955

THE GARRICK THEATRE, LORD ST, SOUTHPORT

Morton Fraser's Harmonica Gang and Glady Morgan and Company, head the Garrick Theatre's variety bill next week. There is a fine supporting group of artistes - many voiced Peter Sellers, Lee Young, Wilson Keppel and Betty, The Three Balmorals, Reg Daponte and the Hill Billy Polecats. This should be a show worth seeing.

Southport Guardian 14th September 1955

REVIEW

Direct from GOONLAND comes Peter Sellers. His patter intermingled with character impressions such as those of Henry Crum and Minnie is rich fare.

Impressions of famous personalities including Sir Winston Churchill form another feature of his bright and breezy act.

Southport Visiter 30th March 2001

Look Back – Memories from a bygone time

by Phil Coghlan

FOLLOWING last week's feature on the Palace Hotel, I had a great response from readers wanting to share happy memories of times spent there.

Nola Nelson, a former teacher from Southport, used to go ballroom dancing at the Palace hotel in the 1960's as it offered an alternative to the Floral Hall. The floor was taken from the Palais de Dance, which was on the site of Woolworths. Mrs Nelson was lucky enough to meet Clark Gable outside the hotel during his stay.

Elsie Mansergh, of Faulkner Close, used to work at the hotel serving afternoon teas and getting the suites ready for guests. She was employed from time to time when there were large banquets on. During her years at the hotel she served many famous guests with tea and earned ten shillings for four hours work.

The stars stayed at the hotel while they were appearing at the Garrick Theatre. Now Mecca Bingo, Lord Street. Among the guests she met were Anne Shelton, Derel Roy and Ted Ray who used to judge the English Rose. Each star appearing at the Garrick always did.

When serving Peter Sellers he asked Mrs Mansergh if she had any binoculars he could borrow so that he could see the sea from his bedroom!

Mrs Mansergh said: "Along the way that's another gracious building gone. Not much old world charm left now, as they say, for us grandmothers. But along with the lovely Prince of Wales it was the crème de la crème of hotels."

A possible visit from Charlie Chaplin

Full Name : Charles Spencer Chaplin
Date & Place of Birth : 16th April 1889, London
Possible year of visit : 1908   Age : 18

Background to visit :

If Charlie Chaplin hadn't had a caring brother, we might never have seen one the greatest comedic talents, Britain has ever produced.

It is well-documented that Charlie Chaplin, only got his opportunity in show business, through the intervention of his brother (I call it 'pestering').

Sydney Chaplin, already an employee of Fred Karno's entertainment company, continually asked if his younger brother, Charlie, could join.

Fred Karno eventually relented and allowed a very young (16-years-old) Charlie Chaplin to help and perform in Karno's Army.

Karno entertained audiences with a specific brand of comedy. He was a former circus gymnast and pioneer of slapstick comedy.

Karno passed on this physical art to all his performers, which included both Charlie Chaplin and Stan Laurel.

The British Film Institute (BFI) notes that Charlie Chaplin signed a contract with Fred Karno on the 21st February 1908.

This is after Karno's Army comes to the Pier Pavilion in early February. There is a review of Karno's Army in a Southport Visiter newspaper, dated 4th February 1908.

The unfortunate thing for me, as a researcher, is that Chaplin is not mentioned during the performance. There are no references to names or ages of the performers or a cast list to scrutinise.

There is an argument for and against him coming to Southport. More conclusive proof is needed before we can say for sure.

Karno's Army performed at the Pier Pavilion, Promenade, Southport.

SOUTHPORT. PIER PAVILION.

Here is a postcard of the now demolished, Pier Pavilion, The Promenade, Southport.

Anthony Quayle

Full Name : John Anthony Quayle
Date & Place of Birth : 7th September 1913 - Ainsdale, Southport
UK

Background :

Anthony Quayle was born in Ainsdale, in a house on Delamere Road. He realised while boarding at Rugby School in Warwickshire, he wasn't cut out for an academic life.

Instead he set his sights on becoming an actor, causing his family much concern. How was he going to survive when he left school?

They need not have worried. Quayle left Southport to embark on an extraordinary film and stage career.

Quayle often played military men on the silver screen with great realism and depth. This might be due to the fact that Quayle fought in the Second World War. Taking method acting to a new extreme.

He was an excellent soldier and joined the fore-runner of modern special forces, the S.O.E. (Special Operations Executive).

After the war, Quayle resumed his acting career.

Starring in classic films such Ice Cold In Alex (1958)(For which Quayle received a BAFTA nomination), The Guns of Navarone (1961)(A multiple Oscar-winning film) and Lawrence of Arabia (1962) (Only won seven Oscars...), Quayle became a worldwide star.

In 1970, Quayle was nominated for an Oscar, for his portrayal of Cardinal Wolsey, opposite Richard Burton's King Henry VIII in Anne of a Thousand Days. Sadly Quayle just missed out to surprise winner, Gig Young.

In 1985, Quayle got a richly deserved knighthood. Four years later, in 1989, halfway through his autobiography "A Time To Speak," Quayle discovered he was terminally ill with liver cancer. Knowing full well he only had a short time left to live, Quayle bravely carried on and completed writing his life story.

Thankfully great actors never truly die. They live on, immortalised in film.

Miranda Richardson

MIRANDA RICHARDSON (Jude) in Neil Jordan's **THE CRYING GAME.**

PolyGram

Filmed Entertainment

Full Name : Miranda Richardson
Date & Place of Birth : 3rd March 1958, Southport,UK

Background :

Miranda Richardson knew exactly what she wanted to be, when she left school (Southport High School for Girls now Greenbank High School). She wanted to be an actress.

Unfortunately at the time, studying Drama did not merit an education grant from the local authority.

Richardson didn't let her dream of acting die, though. It would have been very easy to give up and do something mundane. A determined Richardson wasn't going to give up and wonder, "What if....?" for the rest of her life.

Instead she bravely left for the Bristol Old Vic Theatre School. After 3 years, she had completed the acting drama course. Again, her search for professional excellence didn't stop there.

Richardson then went to expand her acting experience at the Library Theatre in Manchester. All the time Richardson evolved as an actress. Richardson then travelled to the bright lights of London to do stage work.

As with many acting careers, there is a gradual progression. Richardson then got small parts on television in the early 1980s. In 1985, she made the film,

"Dance With A Stranger," which showcased Richardson's undeniable acting talent. It was a demanding part for Richardson, who deftly portrayed Ruth Ellis. Ellis was the last woman to be hanged in the UK for murdering her lover.

Richardson then participated in both television parts and film roles, such was the demand for her talent. She is very well known for her role as Queen Elizabeth I in the BBC comedy, Blackadder. Again, Richardson demonstrated her chameleon-like acting ability. Not only could she do harrowing scenes in Dance With A Stranger, she also excelled in comedy. You name the genre, Richardson could do it all.

In 1987, Richardson starred in Steven Spielberg's award winning film, Empire of the Sun. In 1992, she was part of an Oscar winning film called The Crying Game.

In 1999, she was a main character in the Oscar winning film, Sleepy Hollow, playing opposite Johnny Depp. In 2000, she starred in Get Carter opposite Sylvester Stallone.

In 2005, she made Wah Wah with Gabriel Byrne. Not to mention Harry Potter and the Goblet of Fire in 2005 playing the part of Rita Skeeter.

Richardson continues to make television drama and films. Long may she continue. She is undoubtedly, a great British actress.

Newspaper coverage:-

<u>Southport Visiter Friday 18th January 1985</u>

Miranda on brink of stardom

The career of Southport-born actress Miranda Richardson looks likely to take a major leap forward as a result of her film debut performance as Ruth Ellis, the last Englishwoman to be hanged. Of her portrayal as the ex-club hostess who murders her upper class lover in "Dance with a Stranger," which goes on general release in March, one critic wrote: "From the sheer virtuosity of her performance, you would think she had been a major screen actress for years."

Says another: "Her portrayal of the vulnerable, confused and love-stricken heroine is one of the most sensational screen debuts of recent years!"

Although Miranda now shares a London flat with another former Bristol Old Vic actress, her proud parents still live in Lord Street. Explains her mother, Marian: "The film only covers the two years ending with the death of Blakely (played by Rupert Everett) and I'm thankful it didn't include the subsequent trial and execution." About 150 other actresses are believed to have been eager to try for the part, but Miranda's father, Mr. Alan Richardson – a keen member of the Friends of the Art Centre – thinks it was the rave reviews she earned for her portrayal of Marilyn Monroe in the Bristol Old Vic production of "Insignificance" which caught the attention of film director Mike Newell, although he admits: "Quite honestly, I couldn't see my daughter being brassy enough to play Ruth Ellis."

Miranda will be 27 in March, and it was her appearance in two plays at Southport High School for Girls which brought her to the attention of Southport Dramatic Club, for who she starred in the "Cinderella," pantomime and took part in a couple of other productions.

Then it was on to a scheduled three-year drama course with the Bristol Old Vic Theatre School, but Miranda was one of three youngsters who progressed so well that she completed the course in two years.

She then joined the Manchester Library Theatre, playing a leading role in her first play, "Tom Jones," and staying for a season, which also included "Play it again Sam."

Around this time, Miranda broke into TV advertising and for three years she was Yardley's Christmas girl.

More importantly, she got her first West End chance playing Penelope Keith's daughter in "Moving" – transferred only last week to TV with Penelope again starring – which was staged at the Queen's Theatre with Peter Jeffrey and Barbara Ferris also in the cast.

Since that first film role, Miranda has appeared in Granada's "Crown Court" series, played one of Deborah Kerr's granddaughters in TV's "Woman of Substance" and has filmed "Demon Lover" with Dorothy Tutin and "The Innocent" shot around Settle.

She is currently considering other offers.

Films shot in Southport

Southport hasn't just been a town where stars have visited or performed. The town itself has provided the location for several films, which have all had a nationwide cinema release.
Below is a collection of newspaper articles relating to films shot in the resort.

Study in Scarlet (1914)

Blue Peter (1928)

Combat America (1944)

Forbidden Cargo / Custom's Story (1954)

What's Good For The Goose (1969)

The Haunted House of Horror / The Dark (1969)

Slayground (1983)

Mr. Love (1985)

A Study in Scarlet (1914)

The Southport Guardian 27th June 1914

A NOVEL SCENE

MANUFACTURING FILMS ON BIRKDALE SANDHILLS

'A STUDY IN SCARLET' TABLEAU

359 people, 60 horses, 15 wagons, a flock of sheep, and a herd of cattle were engaged in the manufacture of a section of film for Messrs. The Samuelson Film Manufacturing Co. Ltd of Isleworth, on Birkdale sandhills, close to the termination of Trafalgar Road, during yesterday.

The work in hand was the depicting of that portion of Sir Arthur Conan Doyle's "A Study in Scarlet," where Brigham Young and his band of Mormon cross the Alkali Plain before arriving at the place which ultimately became Salt Lake City.

Imagination, we have been told, has no boundaries, and so, although in reality we traversed Trafalgar Road, Birkdale, and came on to the sandhills, we imagined we were on the great Alkali Plain, an arid and repulsive desert, almost barren, inhospitable and miserable. We had made numerous enquiries amongst the Geographical Departments in London as to the nature of the ground in different parts of England; in fact we had made a thorough search of the country, but these sandhills with the peculiarity of their formation, the soft, fine sand, and the tufts of grass, were the nearest approach to that we desirous of representing.

A day or two before we had been on the Cheddar Hills, busy with scenes in the Rocky Mountains.

We had also been engaged in other places, and now Birkdale sandhills were to provide the base for an interesting and essential connecting link. Some of us arrived on Thursday, including Mr. H. Engholm, the secretary and editor of the company of which by the way, Mr. G.B. Samuelson, a native of Southport, is the managing director, 18 cinema actors and actresses from London, and other officials. An early start was made with the preliminary details and men were engaged converting ordinary wagons into caravans. Passers-by were curious as to the proceedings but their curiosity was not satisfied. Still such a novelty could not be kept secret in the main, because the 359 "supers" had friends whom they must tell of their decision to become Mormons for a few hours, and so at seven o'clock yesterday morning the query, "Are you a Mormon?" was heard so frequently that it became quite familiar. Everything should have been ready for a start at the hour named, but the arrangements were not carried out with unblemished precision, and therefore it was much later here the trek was actually accomplished. It was with considerable difficulty (writes a "Southport Guardian" representative) that the 60 horses managed to haul the 15 canvas-covered wagons to the crest of the hills. While some previously engaged workmen were pursuing this task other local people were being enrolled as temporary Mormons, and as the pay was good, and the work entailed slight, there was no lack of volunteers.

They, too, proceeded, to the crest of the hills, to where the caravans had finally been placed. We were very anxious that the portrayal of this famous trek of Brigham Young, with his 10,000 Mormons, should be as realistic as possible, and so great attention had to be paid to numerous small things, and a long, tedious wait for most of us ensued; indeed, the marshalling took hours, and the actual trek minutes – that was the actual worst part of it from the spectators' point of view.

At last a voice rings forth, "Are you ready?" the answering call, "yes," is heard, a bell rings, and the trek has started. We imagine that the caravans have come from far far away on the extreme verge of the Alkali Plain, and that a little spray of dust, hardly distinguishable from the mists of the district, has grown, and grown until after making certain that it can only be caused by a multitude of moving creatures, we see cattle and sheep at the head of the column, followed by figures of horsemen , tired worn people trailing along at either side of the vehicles and children looking tired and pale as they peer from the arched doorways cut in the canvas. Brigham Young, (Harry Paulo, a famous old clown) we notice, is seated at the front of the second wagon, interested in a large book which he holds in his hands. Suddenly an exclamation is uttered by one of the keenest eyed of the party. He is on horseback, goes forward, and discovers a man ("John Ferrier," Mr. Le Fre) dying from hunger and thirst and a little child.

("Lucy"). The former is assisted and the latter is carried to Brigham Young, the Mormons crowd around them, for the caravan has come to a halt.

Brigham Young, after consideration, gives directions to his elders, to take care of the man and child, orders to proceed, and this is done. The motley crowd, we imagine, have passed out of our range of vision, and have halted at Brigham Young's "Land of Promise."

The actual trek has not been of long duration, but much money has been spent to make it possible, between £100 and £200 and it is a reminder of the difficulties of film manufacturers have to contend with, for they find it necessary to visit many places to make one complete film.

In "A Study in Scarlet" Mr. Sherlock Holmes is introduced to the public for the first time. Messrs The Samuelson Film Manufacturing Co.Ltd, searched England for a man who in appearance was like the famous Sherlock Holmes was supposed to be, and they were at last very fortunate, for so good is the likeness between the actor who takes the role and Sherlock Holmes, that the Company do not consider it necessary to inform the public by letterpress when the impersonation of the character of Sherlock Holmes is about to be thrown on the screen at picture theatres.

They had a further difficulty in finding a man for like Brigham Young – a fine looking man of stern countenance. They interviewed over 100 persons before they secured one who, in addition to being of suitable appearance, also possessed ability to act well.

One of the reasons the Samson films – those manufactured by the Samuelson Co. – are so expensive is that only copyright works are undertaken. In the ordinary way, manufacturers endeavour to obtain stories which can be told in picture form after expenditure on the most economical lines. With copyright works the ideas of the authors must be followed in much detail, otherwise the realistic touch is absent.

Blue Peter (1928)

Southport Visiter 26th May 1928

Filming African Scenes at Ainsdale

Local interest in the preparation

Mr. Matheson Lang

The African scenes of the film, "The Blue Peter," based on the play written by Mr. Temple Thurston, are to be taken on the Ainsdale Sandhills. Yesterday afternoon, I found a considerable crowd of people in the vicinity of the scene, the preparation of which was nearing completion.

There were quite a number of school girls and boys and snapshot cameras were busy.

After turning off Shore Road, the ground became so hilly that I had to leave my bicycle by a hill near the bungalow, which in the picture will be occupied by the engineers and others directing the mine.

The shaft head of this is close by, and towards it run little railway lines on which are bogey trucks. There is also a thatch-covered hut, which is a "pay-box" where the natives receive the reward of their labour. The windows of the bungalow have been so constructed that guns can be, in the terse phrase of my informant, "shoved through," when the bungalow is attacked by natives. This is, of course, only one of the many scenes to be filmed.

After traversing a fair stretch of sandhill, I came to the wonderful "facsimile" of a Nigerian kraal, which has been erected.

It is from here that the natives will set out to attack. Experts have been consulted, and the Colonial Office has given every assistance, so that everything shall be correct. Mr. Arthur Rooke, the producer paid a high tribute to Mr.Harry Harrison, under whose direction the building, etc. had been done, and who had applied the expert knowledge gained so faithfully.

Wonderful was the scene as we stood near the beginning of the village "street."

The native huts, some mud and some of cane and all thatched with straw, were close together, those furthest away being on slightly rising ground.

Mr. Rooke contradicted the statement which gained currency that lions and tigers were going to be brought down.

There will be only such animals as ponies for the white men (who will be rounding up the pagan natives), goats and bullocks and a bullock cart will be seen about the village.

As we made our way along the "street" the perfection of detail noted was remarkable.

I looked at the quaint little entrance to the mud huts, and I should have thought they had been there for years if I had not known the sandhills without them.

It had been impossible to get stones just like those in Nigeria, so some had been specially manufactured, and these were to be seen near the huts.

Mr. Harrison made a short pause in his directing operations, and brought a cup of tea for a young lady who was with Mr. Rooke and his friends, and remarked "Straight from the Walla wallas," whatever that might mean.

Mr Rooke was about to tell me how to spell "kraal," when I said, "You need not. I remember the Boer War."

"So do I," replied Mr. Rooke, "I was playing in "The Silver King" at the Southport Opera House when the news of the relief of Mafeking came through, and I will never forget the scene."

Mr. Harrison, too, had his tribute to pay in connection to the work carried out. They had, he said, been able to give work to a considerable number of the local unemployed giving preference to ex-servicemen. Without exception, they were good and conscientious workers and if he came to the district at some future time to construct for another film, he would employ again as many of them as were available.

Many printed notices worded as follows were ready to be put up "This ground is private." "The Public will assist the producer of the picture if they will please keep outside the ropes."

The Chief Constable of Southport (Major Egan) visited the village yesterday afternoon.

Some interesting particulars were given by Mr. Rooke to the "Liverpool Post" cinema correspondent in London.

Southport Guardian June 2nd 1928

Autograph hunters and Picnic Parties

So great is the attraction provided for residents of Southport and district, as well as holiday visitors, in the making of the film "The Blue Peter," based on Mr Temple Thurston's play, that not only do they flock in crowds to Ainsdale sandhills, but many go in picnic parties, so as to be on the spot and not miss any interesting adventure which is in progress of being "shot."

They trek over the sandhills that lie on the left of the Shore Road, the one that goes down to the beach.

The high sandhills provide many a point of vantage, so that it is possible to obtain an excellent view of all that is going on.

A full description of the setting has already appeared in these columns, and to the same have come a score or so of African natives, men and women with gaudy loin cloths, robes and attire of a non-descript nature which recalls an old nigger minstrel joke. "These are my summer clothes. Some are clothes, and some are not clothes." And real summer weather came so that the natives revel in the almost tropical temperatures, while the white members of the cast perspire to such an extent that there is for the spectators that peculiar pleasure which comes from being able to sit quiet and restful watching others who are "hot and bothered."

To London for interiors

The various incidents in the story filmed will be woven into the general scheme of things. The filming will continue to the end of the week, when the company will go to London to do "interiors" returning to Ainsdale about three weeks later.

The natives who respond with vim to the suggestions of Mr. Arthur Rooke, the producer. They like their work so much that their countenances appear to shine with even greater delight when the instructions of the producer have not been understood by them in the first instance and they have to do it all over again. Sometimes "shot" after "shot" has to be taken to get an incident, so that the spectators get plenty of amusement arising out the producer's difficulties.

One incident is the welcome of the villagers to the new governor, David Hunter (the principal part played by Mr. Matheson Lang). The natives ran in from the hills to the bungalow with smiling faces and hearty cries of greeting. Mr Lang came down the sandy hill to the mining headquarters in a rude cart drawn through the heavy sand by a horse driven by a native boy in khaki. The animal if it had not the ancestry of a mule, had evidently acquired some mulish characteristics.

Two or three times the conveyance got within a few yards of its destination, and then there was a sort of back-pedalling performance, with disconcerting effects on Mr. Lang and his luggage.

However, this did not materially affect the work in hand, and Mr. Lang, clad in cool grey drill and wearing a topi, was welcomed not only by the natives, but also in mining engineers dressed in khaki, with revolvers strapped to their waists.

Mr. Lang and other members of the company were constantly "snap-shotted."

He posed for one little girl in various positions until she had used all her "films."

Another girl had taken up to Mr. Lang a folded sheet on the front of which was written "Ainsdale, May, 1928. Lest we forget."

Mr. Lang and Mr. Cameron Carr, who are also taking part in the film, autographed it on the reverse side and the girl's parents were disappointed.

"Thee go back and get 'im to put it on t'reight side," ordered her mother, and away she went to return smilingly triumphant.

Mr. Lang regards the place as a splendid location for the story, but he says, the crowds make the work difficult, especially when there is a call for intimate acting.

The natives have not shown the slightest embarrassment and the crowds have finely responded to Mr. Rooke's appeal to have regard to any sensitiveness they might feel. In one scene at the Nigerian kraal, Mr. Matheson Lang was photographed riding a large grey horse. A number of tom-toms, native images and shields were brought to the village. These scenes lead up to the point where the natives make an attack on the bungalow, as outlined in last Saturday's "Southport Guardian."

No second Hollywood probable at Ainsdale

These films doings have naturally caused people to ask whether there is any probability of a second Hollywood springing up in the Merseyside area.

On this point a "Liverpool Post" representative sought the views of Mr. H.W.May; manager the British Filmcraft Production Company, who has been in the British film business since 1912, and who is in charge of the work at Ainsdale.

"I'm afraid it will be a long time before we see any film studios in the North," said Mr. May.

"They tend to concentrate more and more in the London area for obvious reasons. The centre of the film business is there and so are all the agents who matter. You must do business through the agents. Again, London is the rallying place for film actors and actresses. These we can engage, as we require them for a picture and get the benefit of their services quickly in a London studio.

"It would be stupid to inaugurate a film studio, for instance, in Ainsdale, when all sorts of queries and business would have to be done through London, with resulting delay and expense. Then the selling end of the British film industry is in London, and the film Press as well. We could hardly expect the London film press to follow our pictures through the early stages if we buried our studio away in the North.

"Again, if we need an experienced crowd of extras, London is the only place where we can get hold of them quickly. It would increase our overhead expenses tremendously in railway fares alone if we had to bring say 200 people up to Southport for a production. In our present production we are lucky in being able to obtain several hundred coloured people from Merseyside dockland, but in other productions we might not be so fortunate."

It was not merely a question of light, continued Mr. May, Studios were established mainly for indoor work, and if special scenes were needed a film company was quite willing to seek them in any part of the country.

Electricity also played a great part in establishing a studio. A very large voltage was needed, and if a studio were established in an out of the way place, it would mean expensive installation.

The British film industry has its eye on the Continent according to Mr. May, where there are huge potential markets for good British films. British film companies were going more and more on the Continent to complete sets. His company was going to Belgium shortly to film Masterlinck's "Burgomaster of Stilemonde." It would be far more convenient to handle a production like this from London than from a studio in the North of England.

A film colony will never grow naturally here in the Liverpool district or anywhere else outside the London radius. The only way such a colony could be started would be for several new companies with large capital yet to be spent on location to build studios here. The rest might then follow, but it would be impossible for any individual company to make that move.

Forbidden Cargo (1954)

Southport Visiter 19th September 1953

SOUTHPORT IN NEW FILM

SMUGGLING SCENES ON SHORE

Arrangements have been made with the J. Arthur Rank Production Ltd. to visit Southport for five or six days commencing September 28, to shoot some scenes for a new film on the sand dunes and beach near the Palace Hotel.

The film, "The Custom's story," will include smuggling scenes with tank landing craft and lorries.

The previous occasion when shots were taken on the Southport sands was in 1928 when the film, "The Blue Peter," was being produced by Matheson Lang.

FILM MEN WON'T NEED 'EXTRAS'

STARS NOT COMING TO SOUTHPORT

Any starry-eyed Southport youngsters who imagined that they would be able to break into film acting as the result of a visit a unit of the J.Arthur Rank Organisation is to pay here next week, had their hopes dashed yesterday.

An official of the organisation, speaking from London, told the Visiter that the unit would need no extras.

The only local man who will appear in the film will be one of the D.U.K.W. drivers of Mr. J.Rankin of Churchtown, who operates the amphibious fleet here for rescue work and pleasure trips during the season.

The film entitled, "The Custom's Story," is all about dope smuggling on the British coast. The shots made in Southport will be purely scenic background views.

"It will be meant simply to represent some part of the British coast, not any particular part," said the official. Further shots will later be made in the South of France. The stars of the film, Nigel Patrick and Jack Morgan will not be present but director Harold French, who was responsible for the film,

"Encore," will come to Southport.

Mr. Rankin told the Visiter that the film organisation had contacted him and ordered a D.U.K.W. painted battleship gray, complete with driver.

He has been told that it will be required on Wednesday and Thursday and possibly Friday. As none of his vehicles are at present this colour, he has had to make the alteration.

Southport Visiter 1st October 1953

WEATHER DELAYS FILMING

FIVE SHOTS OBTAINED SO FAR

In between showers, members of the J.Arthur Rank Film unit, on location in Southport for, "The Custom's Story," spent most of yesterday feeding seagulls. While it rained they stayed in their cars near Birkdale sandhills.

"It was a completely blank day," said the production manager, Mr. Douglas Pierce. "We were in the cars from 8:30 in the morning until 3:30 in the afternoon."

The unit who came to town on Monday are scheduled to stay five days. This period will have to be extended if the rain persists.

"We are not really worried but there are certain shots which we simply have to take," said Mr Pierce.

Chief among these is a scene showing a D.U.K.W. smuggling 'narcotics' ashore to a waiting lorry.

The deadline for completion of the Southport scene is October 11th, when the unit will fly to Cannes in the South of France. Members are not unduly perturbed about the weather here.

"Most of us have been through worse delays," said Mr. Pierce. "The technique is to wait for even the briefest period of sunshine and then move as fast as you possibly can."

On Tuesday, the unit managed to secure five shots, despite a strong wind and the fact that although the day was clear, there was little sunshine. When the D.U.K.W. scene is ultimately filmed the driver will be Mr. Joseph Rankin and loading the narcotics into the waiting lorry will be five of his men.

Southport Visiter 3rd October 1953

WORKLESS USED AS FILM EXTRAS

UNIT MOVES TO FORMBY TODAY

The J.Arthur Rank Film unit which arrived here on Monday to shoot scenes for, "The Custom's Story," picked local 'extras' yesterday from the unemployed list at the Labour Exchange. The Exchange's clientele will feature in the film as prosperous Customs officials and not so prosperous lookers during a scene in which a D.U.K.W., manned by Mr. Arthur Rankin and five of his employees move ashore with a load of contraband.

"We had the extras sweeping around in cars and generally lending atmosphere to the scene," Production manager, Mr. Douglas Pierce told the Visiter yesterday.

Early today the unit will forsake it's Birkdale location and move down to Formby close by the Coastguard's post for further filming.

"The tides here at Southport have been something of a handicap," said Mr. Pierce.

"In Formby there are deep inshore channels which will enable us to shoot the D.U.K.W. coming straight out of the water to the top of the beach instead of having to go several hundred yards to the point of unloading."

Southport Visiter 5th June 1954

SOUTHPORT ON THE SCREEN

FORBIDDEN CARGO FILM ARRIVES

Scenes shot in the Southport area earlier in the year will be shown on the Grand cinema screen when the film, "Forbidden Cargo," starts a week's run tomorrow. This is a story about smuggling and the film studio decided to make coastal scenes at

Southport and Formby as the coast here resembles an area in France, where the story is set.

One of the people in Southport most keenly looking forward to seeing the film is Mr. Ken Sumner, of Broughton Avenue, who went on location with the film makers and acted as stand in for one of the stars.

He had to play the role of skipper of a contraband ship, coming ashore in a craft in the Formby area.

"It was so realistic that I believe the Customs people saw us and had inquiries made," he told the Visiter yesterday.

What's Good For The Goose (1969)

Southport Journal Visiter 18th July 1968

Norman starts the fun and camera rolling

Holidaymakers, actors, actresses, cameramen, technicians and Norman Wisdom. They all mingled together in the Burton Arcade, Lord Street where shooting began on Norman's new film on Monday. Crowds of autograph hunters and interested onlookers gather round the shop next door to Southport Stationers Ltd which has been taken over by the film company, Tigon British Film Productions Ltd as a modern 'with it' Boutique for one of the scenes in the film.

The film, "What's Good For The Goose" will be shot mainly in Southport and should take around six weeks. This particular scene, shot on Monday will also feature some of Southport's young students who have been engaged as extras for the boutique scene to give it the authentic touch. Norman who is co-producer of the film along with Tony Tenser revealed that other venues had been thought of for the film, such as Bournemouth, Weymouth and Torquay but Southport had come out tops in the end.

"This is my seventeenth film and it is the first time that I've been married in a film.

It's the story of a man around 40 who is dedicated to his work until he is accidentally introduced to a young girl. From then on a new life begins for him."

For the scene shot on Monday the previously wealthy shop was transformed into a very 'gear' boutique full of 'mod' uniforms, cuddly toys and even an old penny farthing. In the scene, Norman who goes to buy a present for his new girlfriend who is played by Sally Geeson, discovers the delights of the boutique and finishes by buying something far more unconventional.

"I am not on holiday," he replied to one questioner who obviously was not fully aware of the rigours involved in film making, "But if I'm working it's like a holiday to me because I enjoy working."

Miss Geeson said that she hadn't worked with Norman before but was looking forward to it. "It should be marvellous," she added. The film is expected to cost around £200,000 and will be in Technicolor. Much of it will be set on Southport's beaches and it is expected that the film will be released towards the end of the year.

Southport Visiter 20th July 1968

Southport Had Just Everything

The person responsible for bringing the film, "What's Good For The Goose" on location to Southport was the star of the film himself, Norman Wisdom. Norman, dressed in unfamiliarly smart morning suit took a few moments off from a tight shooting schedule to explain how this happened.

"We needed a seaside town and everyone was discussing Brighton, Southend and so on. Then I suggested Southport." Norman added that he knew the town well having stayed here several years ago while appearing in the pantomime "Robinson Crusoe" at Liverpool. His first visit here was in 1949 when he clowned in variety at the Garrick Theatre.

"We came here to have a look at Southport and it seemed to have everything we wanted," he said. "There was a large hotel, The Palace, with everything we needed.

It was even empty and available for use. Then there were the marvellous sand dunes and Pleasureland, so here we are." He added, "Everyone has been marvellous and we have had co-operation everywhere especially from your corporation who have been most helpful."

West Lancashire Visiter 23rd July 1968

Wisdom of Norman - he is no fool

Shooting scenes in the heart of Southport surrounded by swarms of holidaymakers, children and autograph hunters can't be easy but Norman Wisdom finds time to sign all books, envelopes and scraps of paper thrust at him. He even finds the energy for impromptu clowning for the benefit of the crowds.

However beneath all the fooling there is a serious and very professional person, a man who has obviously studied himself, his aims in showbusiness and his roles. "The public today is not satisfied with straightforward comedy. Also, I have always wanted to act because I can act.

For years I have done knock about comedy which I love and which I'll do again but when I expressed an interest in doing the Jack Lemmon style of comedy, people only laughed."

It took a visit to the United States to prove to others that he could do this other more subtle form of comedy. Norman won two Broadway awards for his playing in the musical version of "Hobson's Choice," and then went on

to make a colour television version of "Androcles and the Lion," with Noel Coward.

"I could have walked around Britain with the back hanging out of my trousers before anyone offered me roles like that," he commented.

In a very serious vein, Norman said, "I want to do what I want to do. I'll be damned if I go back to my original style," He is not however nursing any secret ambition to be a Hamlet.

Norman has always insisted on doing what he feels is right. Back at the beginnings of his comedy career he wanted to play the clarinet and sing as part of his act. "They wouldn't have it. I was told that if they wanted a clarinet player they could get twenty. If they wanted a singer they could hire one. I stuck it out then and I'll stick it out now," Norman, together with the director,

Menachem Golan, has written the script for "What's Good For The Goose."

The story concerns an assistant bank manager who suddenly realises that life has slipped him by.

The world of the younger generation with its pop music, hippy clothes and different attitudes suddenly hits him and he wants to join in this brave new world before it is too late. "This is not really a change in style for me but the film is a different type. This is more sincere with more depth than my previous films which had carried a light story line. Here I fall in love which is ridiculous as I'm 40 years old now. It is also a bit sexy and I've never done this before,"

Norman did not see any parallel between his film character and himself.

"Unlike the bank manager who thinks he has missed out on all this hippy gear and so on it just doesn't appeal to me. I have not missed out on the things I enjoy in life, things like music, athletics, car racing and sport," Away from the roar of the crowds and smell of the greasepaint what does Norman do with his time? His first stop will be a football ground to watch the match. A devoted fan, he is director of Brighton and Hove Albion.

Southport has a new hotel. It's slightly odd and unexpected. I would not advise you to book in but if you manage to do so via the false switchboard there is every likelihood that your bedroom will be illuminated suddenly and brilliantly from a ceiling full of strong spotlights.

Failing this you could encounter unlikely objects at every turn of the corridors such as the scarlet lavatory seat with matching geranium growing from it or a roomful of hippy flower shirts or cases of dark Egyptian pancake make-up.

The bar of this hotel, the Grand Hotel is likely to be untended and the walls could be false.

You might also have reservations about the casual way in which the members of the staff are dressed. The men seem to favour knotted cravats, long hair and corduroy and the women micro mini skirts or gay trouser suits.

Beneath the wrist thick cables, piled up basket chairs and studio lamp stands, any Southport visitor could still detect shades of the Victorian splendour of the Palace Hotel, Birkdale. This has now been taken over by the Tigon British Films Production Limited unit for Norman Wisdom's new film, "What's Good For The Goose," In the Past, The Palace Hotel has coped with conferences, dances and the accommodation and comfort of delegates, so it was no surprise to hear George Mills, the productions manager say that the hotel is proving to be idea for the film. It's type casting. The Palace is playing a conference hotel. A few theatrical touches have been added to the old lady. The former "Ladies Room" sign now reads, "Make-Up Room," and the mirrors are framed with the traditional unflattering glare of naked light bulbs.

Bottles of acetone and orange tins of leichner stage powder are neatly stacked out; a sign that make up is part of the business, not a feminine extravagance.

Extravagance takes over in the ballroom where a special conference table has been built by construction manager Lou Sayers and his team.

This oval table big enough to skate across is so impressively outsize it would terrify any normal delegate.

It has been constructed not only for effect but to hold the camera while it dollies from a close up of a cigar back to a full length shot of the actors.

The biggest job now is being tackled by art director Hayden Pearce who is designing the discotheque, a scene which will include many Southport extras. He and assistant Peter Williams are planning this for the sunless acres of basement below the hotel. However I found them taking advantage of the sunny gardens out front, in which to sound out ideas and sketch plans. They had just decided on the theme. The discotheque is to be called the Screaming Apple. "We're planning that half the room will be in the form of an enormous apple with jaws. Inside this will be the bar," explained Hayden Pearce, who admitted that he was enjoying thinking out schemes for the way out pop scenes. To date he has designed the pop art shop "Heatwave" (where the red lavatory seat was the piece de resistance) and the boutique on Lord Street. "We borrowed paintings and other art stuff from the art school and one student ended up as an extra on the film," added Mr.Pearce.

One bedroom has been taken over as surprisingly enough, a bedroom.

Even a comparatively simple set like this has had to be altered.
The wall has been extended and a false one built behind the bed.
This is to enable a camera to take shots from behind Norman
Wisdom's head. Hanging heavily over the entire room are tons of
lamps, darkened when I was there, awaiting the star.

Norman Wisdom and the unit were at that moment taking
advantage of the sunshine at Pleasureland.

Despite the hustle and air of gaiety which surrounded the extras
and onlookers, it wasn't all the fun of the fair for the stars.

Norman, all prepared to slide down the helter skelter was forced
to sit on top for the next half hour while the technicians hurriedly
prepared lighting for the gloomy landing strip.

Southport Visiter 3rd August 1968

She loves to laugh

How thoroughly refreshing, to meet a teenager and a well-known
one at that, who's quite happy with life and minus any fermenting
complexes. Eighteen-year-old Sally Geeson, one of the leading
stars in "What's Good For The Goose" now being filmed in
Southport with Norman Wisdom, is such a personality.

In her looks there is something of the early Bridgette Bardot about
her tousled hair and wide awake eyes and although she looks
very feminine she admitted to being a country girl born and bred
and far more at home in a pretty white polo sweater and pale blue

jeans than sophisticated clothes. She is a girl who loves to laugh. "I really enjoy comedy parts like this one," she smiled.

"I always ask Norman to say something funny before the scene and usually it is so hilarious that I almost dry up during the 'shooting'."

Her role as Nikki calls for a wild young and gay personality and in order to project herself into the role she has even taken to walking along Lord Street in her bare feet. She loves Southport and would love to do some horse riding along the beach but unfortunately she hurt her leg slightly during a recent filming incident. At the moment Sally who has no great yearnings for fast cars and other luxury trappings is content to work and keep in work.

Haunted House of Horror (1969)

Southport Visiter 26th October 1968

King of horror comes to resort The film makers are back...!

Tigon British Films returned to Southport this week to make their second film at the temporarily converted studios at The Birkdale Palace Hotel. In contrast to their last film a comedy starring Norman Wisdom their latest, entitled, "The Dark" is a modern suspense story. It is to star the King of horror himself, Boris Karloff, who will arrive in Southport for shooting at the beginning of next week. Also in the line up is Frankie Avalon who will fly from the USA tomorrow, British singing star Mark Wynter and Jill Hayworth whose face is well known to American television viewers. Shooting of the film is scheduled to start on Monday and on arrival at the Birkdale Palace studios yesterday I found construction staff busily preparing sets for the day. T could not help thinking that the Palace had this time undergone a great change for now it has been a luxury hotel in its own right, a luxury hotel on celluloid and now the interior of a haunted house.

The story is a good one but since I have been warned not to give too much of it away and endanger the chastity of suspense, I can only say this, that it concerns a crowd of youngsters who find that they are short of something to do.

One of them has the bright idea of visiting an old house that is supposed to be haunted and thereby hangs the tale.

What I can tell you is that there are plenty of thrills in "The Dark" and that there is at least one bloody murder. You can rest quite assured that true to form, Boris Karloff plays an important role particularly where foul play is indicated. Although much of the actual filming will be done at the Birkdale Palace Hotel Studios some of it will be done on location at Bank Hall on Lord Lilford's estate at Bretherton. This 17th century building has been well chosen for approaching it I could almost hear owls hooting, mist rising and chains clanking, it is so typical of a haunted house.

The film is being made in conjunction with A.I.P. and is assured of a large American market. It is written and directed by Michael Armstrong and is produced by Louis Heyward. Tony Tenser is the Executive Producer and the Art Director is Hayden Pearce. The cameraman is Jack Atcheler.

West Lancashire Visiter 29th October 1968

Star of horror aged 81 flies in

Now in his 82nd year, film star Boris Karloff will be arriving in Southport this week to star in Tigon British Film Productions latest movie, "The Dark" a suspense thriller. Shooting started yesterday at the company's temporarily converted studios in the Birkdale Palace Hotel where their last film a comedy starring Norman Wisdom was made.

Among the other stars that will be arriving in the town are Mark Wynters, the British singing star. Americans Frankie Avalon and Jill Hayworth have already arrived. "The Dark" is written and directed by Michael Armstrong and is produced by Louis Heyward. The Executive Producer is Tony Tenser and the Art Director is Hayden Pearce. Boris Karloff is well known for his parts in thrillers and tales of the supernatural. Starting his film career in the early 1920's he thrilled early cinema goers with his portrayal of Frankenstein's monster.

Southport Visiter 2nd November 1968

Tigon at The Palace

In the foyer of The Palace Hotel there is a notice pointing "The Banqueting Hall." Follow that notice and you will find a dusty cobwebbed room, its floor strewn with rubble and cables. This is one of the main sets for "The Dark", the suspense thriller now being produced by Tigon British Films. Filming has been going ahead at the Palace all week at the steady rate of four minutes a day (in screen time that is).

In charge of the cameras, the lights and the actors is 23-year-old director, Michael Armstrong, who also wrote the script. In the fiercely competitive world of British film making Michael must be one of the youngest directors ever to be put in charge of a major feature production.

He started in show business by going to theatrical school and then became an actor. He then graduated to producing plays and writing them and has arrived in the world of cinema via short film production. Thus within the space of five or six years, he has achieved a distinction sought after by hundreds of older men that of directing a full scale feature film. It is no easy job. Besides his basic function of aiming the camera, Michael must also give full instructions to his star cast and arrange the lighting to obtain the maximum effect.

And then when the film is 'shot' comes the agonising business of sifting and selecting the available material to make up the final screen image. With a tight schedule to meet and an investment of hundreds of thousands of pounds resting on his talent, there is a great deal of responsibility resting on the young shoulders of Michael Armstrong.

Southport Visiter 9th November 1968

U.S.A. STAR SAYS LORD STREET IS 'VERY PRETTY'

Born in Hove, Sussex, attractive American film star Jill Haworth started her talented career when she was very young and when she could barely walk she was entertaining people with her dancing. Since the tender age of three years she has come a long way in show business and she arrived in Southport this week to star as the leading girl in Tigon Film's latest production, "The Dark".

In it, Miss Haworth plays a girl named Sheila, one of the few characters in the film who does not die at the end.

Like Miss Haworth, Sheila is described as being "extremely talented". Huddled over a cup of coffee and feeling the bite of an English winter, I found Miss Haworth waiting to go on set at Bank Hall Bretherton, the exterior of which is being used as a haunted house.

Chatting to her, I got the feeling that Miss Haworth was quite impressed with Southport, though she pointed out she hardly had time to have a proper look round since she arrived.

"I got here about a week ago and haven't seen much of Southport yet but what I have seen I think is very pretty. I think Lord Street is marvellous, very pretty indeed," said Miss Haworth. She is looking forward to seeing more of the town today for she will be doing a doing a spot of shopping on this, her day off.

Basically a dancer, Miss Haworth has been acting for about six years. She has also made her mark as a singer having just completed a two and a half year run in the Broadway musical hit, "Cabaret". During her eight year stay in the U.S.A., Miss Haworth's face has probably become more well known over there but Southport people may have recognised her in recent episodes of "The F.B.I." "Run For Your Life" and "I Spy".

Shooting of Tigon British Film Production's latest film, "The Dark" described as a psychological thriller has now reached the half way mark and is "bang on schedule".

The executive producer of the film, Mr Tony Tenser, told me this while standing huddled in a damp, cold field in Bretherton. For the company have been using Bank Hall, which is on Lord Lilford's estate at Bretherton, as a haunted house and it is unlikely whether they could have picked a more suitable place.

I visited Bank Hall on Thursday when Tigon were shooting their last scenes of the exterior of the building and were it not for a multitude of equipment, lights and film crew, it could have looked for all the world exactly what Mr Tenser wants it to be, an eerie, spooky, haunted house. one of the stars of the film, Boris Karloff, who is well known for his roles in thrillers has unfortunately been delayed in New York but is expected to arrive in Southport at the beginning of next week. Mr Tenser reports that his appeal for film extras has been so, "overwhelming" that many people eagerly wanting to make their mark on celluloid have had to be turned away. "The Dark" will certainly offer cinema goers plenty and one unusual feature of the film is a gruesome murder with a kukri, the famous knife that must draw blood if drawn from its sheath by a Gurkha.

<u>**Southport Visiter 23rd November 1968**</u>

SILENT STARS IN THE DARK

Figures created by a Southport sculptor will be silent stars in a dramatic scene of Tigon British Film Productions thriller, "The Dark". The sculptures by Mr Arnold Harris of 43a Crescent Road, Birkdale form the background of a chase sequence in which a fear crazed girl, played by blonde American actress Jill Hayworth, runs through The Atkinson Art Gallery.

Powerful lines of the work will highlighted by picturing the figures from different angles. The main shooting of this scene was done Sunday but details of the sculpture are now being photographed at the company's studios in The Palace Hotel, Birkdale.

All except five of the sculptures which were on public exhibition at the Art Gallery at the time have now been transferred to the Wennington Road Branch Library.

The other five are now on permanent loan to the Libraries and Arts Committee, three entitled "Flower people" are on show at the Atkinson Art Gallery, one "La Femme" is in the Central Library and one "The Man" is now on view in Birkdale Library.

Slayground (1983)

Southport Visiter 4th March 1983

Cameras roll on funfair for thriller film scenes
By Fiona Mackay

There's murder, mystery, suspense and a lot of very cold actors to be found at Southport's Pleasureland this week.

The fairground, usually deserted at this time of the year, has been invaded by film crews, Hollywood stars and one or two famous British faces for the making of Thorn EMI Film Productions thriller "Slayground."

The film which stars "E.T." actor, Peter Coyote, Mel Smith, of "Not the Nine O'clock News" fame and international stage and screen star Billie Whitelaw, is being shot on location at Southport, Blackpool, London and on the outskirts of New York.

Scripted by Trevor Preston, from the novel by Donald Westlake, of "Point Blank" repute. "Slayground" is a story of savage revenge, relentless pursuit and cold-blooded murder. It is also the story of man called Stone.

The casting of Stone, a professional criminal who specialises in meticulously planned armed robberies yet hates senseless violence and killings, was no easy matter as he is such a complex character.

Producers John Dark, Gower Ford and director Terry Bedford chose Peter Coyote for the part on the strength of his strong

123

physical presence and undoubted versatility, shown most recently in Steven Spielberg's blockbuster "E.T." and in "Cross Creek," in which he took the lead.

However Coyote is modest of his achievements to date and says it would be quite easy to miss his performance in "E.T." if you were giving it less than your full attention.

Although he has only been in the film business for three years, he has been a stage actor for about 20 and in latter years concentrated on stage direction.

Since moving into films, he has appeared in 12 but the tall, lanky American from San Francisco still wonders at his success.

"Auditions are the worst," he told me while relaxing in between shots on the Southport set.

"I'll walk into a waiting room full of these tough, handsome, intelligent looking guys and I'll say to myself 'God, I wouldn't hire me, I'd hire one of those guys.' I haven't worked out yet what it is they like about me, but I'm certainly not complaining."

The part of Stone is very different from Coyote's last starring role as the romantic lead in "Cross Creek." But he is not too bothered about the type of man he portrays – the thing that matters is whether or not the role is demanding.

"I like to explore characters which are complicated and interesting. Unless you are a superstar and you can't plan on being one – you have very little say on how a character should be developed, because in films, it's really up to the director.

If he doesn't like something he just cuts it out and then re-runs it the way he wants it done. I'd like to carry on learning my trade and move into directing some time in the future," he said.

The producers and director of "Slayground" are convinced they have found an actor who will bring depth and integrity to the many faceted character, of Stone.

In contrast to Stone, his life-long friend Jack Abbatt, a reformed London villain, who owes his life to Stone, is played by funny man Mel Smith who became a household name in "Not the Nine O'clock News" and proved his serious acting ability in the television series "Muck and Brass."

Friends in the film, the two actors also became instant buddies off the set.

"It's wonderful working with Mel as he is so wildly inventive. We are able to trade ideas and we both believe in getting the job done. With him being such a big star in England, I was relieved that we were able to get on so well which is vital for the film as well as making life off the set more enjoyable," Coyote said.

Completing the star line-up is Billie Whitelaw who takes on another challenging character study as Madge, a faded and eccentric owner of an English pleasure beach.

Although the fairground is supposed to be on the East coast, all the sequences will be filmed at Southport and Blackpool.

The "Slayground" team, which has been staying at the Prince of Wales Hotel in Southport, all this week, starts filming in Blackpool on Monday for the next two weeks and if everything goes to plan, "Slayground" could be released by the end of this year. "Slayground" is the first project under a new management team at Thorn EMI films, which includes Verity Lambert, director of production. With its medium-sized budget and Anglo-American cast and locations, "Slayground" is far from a mega-dollar production but still aimed at the international market.

Mr.Love (1985)

<u>Southport Visiter July 13th 1984</u>

A most unamusing fate for Queen Victoria

Adventure of Mr Love light up the town

Local residents might well be wondering why the Promenade has suddenly acquired two new statues, why roads have been closed and why Pleasureland has been fully lit at 4 o'clock in the morning.

The answer to these and many more equally mysterious questions lie with Mr. Love or rather the making of Mr. Love – a new low-budget British film being produced by Enigma film from London.

The actors and film crew, who together number more than 90, have been shooting scenes for the film in and around Southport for the last two weeks.

The usual tranquillity of such places as Hesketh Park, the Floral Hall Gardens and the Promenade has been destroyed by the invasion of cameras, lights, generators and all the usual paraphernalia associated with filmmaking.

A two-minute sequence on the Promenade meant the diversion of traffic for the whole day.

Crew and actors alike inhaled the cool, moist air of the Floral Hall Gardens during the early hours of the morning to film some night time sequences.

The director of the film, Roy Battersby, has paid so much attention to detail that he asked for the lights of Pleasureland to be kept on all night while his team shot scenes on the Promenade. The Classic Cinema was re-named The Broadway, while the crew filmed on Lord Street and extras have been hired from Southport's Job Centre at a charge to the film company of £15 a day each. One mother went to sign her daughter in as an extra and was whisked off to the set herself the following day.

Mr. Love stars Maurice Denham who, with 50 years acting experience is a familiar face both on television and the big screen. Barry Jackson, who recently appeared at Manchester's Royal Exchange Theatre with Julie Walters and Tom Courtenay in "Jumpers," Margaret Tyzack, who, over the last 20 years and more has never been far from our television screens, Linda Marlowe and Tony Melody.

Scripted by Kenneth Eastaugh and produced by Robin Douet and Susan Richards, Mr. Love, which is set in Southport, begins with the untimely death of well-mannered parks gardener Donald Lovelace (Barry Jackson) who, it seems, would have few to mourn him.

However, Donald's funeral brings together an odd assortment of women and begins the speculation, the nudges and winks, which grow into the story of Don Juan masquerading as a mild-mannered municipal gardener.

Even Barbara (Linda Marlowe) a high-class whore, arrives to mourn the passing of the man. The true story of Mr. Love is traced in a retrospective look at the late Donald's "dull" life.

Barry Jackson, who plays the part of Donald, describes himself as essentially a "television actor" although he has had parts in such classic films as Ryan's daughter, Raging Moon and Aces High. He has recently completed his latest film, Shooting party, which features a host of stars including James Mason, Robert Hardy and Sir John Gielgud.

"Generally speaking I'm not a film actor," he told me while relaxing before going on set.

"I'm not usually the sort of person who takes leading roles. I haven't got a 'type' like Clint Eastwood or anyone like that. I'm far too short for a start," he said jokingly.

He is small but he sports a strong muscular frame, which does justice to his gymnastic abilities. Jackson hints at the possibility that he may be very much like the character he plays in Mr. Love. "He's rather quiet, inoffensive character – very near me in a way. He's a very sensitive but quite content until he is exposed to the evils of life when he takes a job as a projectionist and is titillated by the sexy films. He then begins to question his life and wonders whether he's missed something along the way."

Can Jackson relate to the character he is portraying? "I am very interested in human behaviour," he said academically.

"If you can't relate to the character you're playing then you've got a problem. Somehow you've got to overcome that problem the best way you can, but I think I can relate to Donald very well."

For Barry Jackson, whose acting career began at LAMDA, Mr. Love marks at least two milestones in his career. It is the first film of the calibre of Mr.Love that he has ever taken a leading role in, and it is the first time he has ever acted in Southport.

"Southport is a magnificent place," he said. "It is very rare that you get as much co-operation as we've had here. I wish we could finish the film off in Southport, but unfortunately we go to London next week."

The crew finish filming here — where all the outdoor shots have been taken — this weekend and move on to London next week to begin filming the indoor scenes.

"It's been hard work in Southport," said Barry Jackson with a sigh of relief. "I've been in more or less every shot since we started. Today is my first real rest and it feels great."

After filming in London, he said he would like to return home to Somerset for a well-earned rest and take his children on holiday.

Donald's friend, in the film, Theo, is played by Maurice Denham, who became a household name when he was heard on the highly successful Much Binding in the Marsh, which ran on radio for years.

Denham's popularity comes also from the 101 film appearances he made in his acting career, which now spans more than 50 years.

"I've been approached by several people in Southport who have asked to shake my hand," he said. "The people are immensely friendly and I have really enjoyed my time here.

"Southport has been an incredible place and we've been very lucky with the weather."

After such a long time in the industry, how does Mr. Denham cope with the pressures of filming?

"It does get rather tiring, but it's all part of the job," he said.

"Hanging around waiting for the crew to get everything just right before they start filming doesn't bother me, I just chat up the birds – like co-artists," he said with a cheeky grin, looking directly at Linda Marlowe.

He is a man of tremendous wit and great confidence. "Mr. Love is going to be very successful," he concluded.

A pointer to its possible success is the fact that executive producer, David Puttnam, was involved with Chariots of Fire, Greystoke and Local Hero.

Set in the present day, Mr. Love has been written for the screen and if everything goes according to plan, it should be released early next year.

Photo montage of Mr. Love

Donald Lovelace (Barry Jackson) stars as Southport's gentle, legendary gardener in the new romantic comedy from Warner Bros., "MR. LOVE."

Copyright © 1985 Warner Bros. Inc.

Melanie (Julia Deakin), a film-crazed usherette, play-acts with Donald Lovelace in "MR. LOVE," the new romantic comedy from Warner Bros.

Copyright © 1985 Warner Bros Inc.

Doris Lovelace (Marcia Warren), faithful wife of Donald Lovelace in "MR. LOVE,"
a new romantic comedy from Warner Bros.

Esther (Christina Collier), an unmarried mother, forms a tragic relationship with
Donald (Barry Jackson) in "MR. LOVE" from Warner Bros.

133

Theo (Maurice Denham) plays a mischievous drop-out in the new comedy from Warner Bros., "MR. LOVE."

Theo (Maurice Denham) and Barbara (Linda Marlowe), Southport's high-class hooker, pay tribute to "MR. LOVE" released by Warner Bros.

G.B. Samuelson
The pioneer film maker from Southport

39-41 Nevill Street, Southport. Birthplace of G.B.Samuelson

This book would not be complete without celebrating the great G.B. Samuelson.

G.B. Samuelson was a film pioneer, trailblazer and risk-taker, all in the name of making films.

For some reason George Berthold Samuelson didn't want to be a tobacconist, like his father. I can't imagine why.

Instead, he wanted to make films. It is unclear why he pursued this career path. His family had not previously been in show business.

Regardless of this, Samuelson proved to be an expert film maker, producing films that were hugely popular and lucrative too. He started making films when he was just twenty-one and made 109 films between 1914 and 1934. This meant he made an average of five films a year, which is incredible by any production standards. He didn't just fund film productions either, he also directed and wrote some of them.

Filmmaking made Samuelson a very wealthy man and eventually he moved from his humble beginnings in Southport, to Isleworth in London.

He ultimately sold his company, much to his regret but carried on directing films. Samuelson made the majority of his films in the silent era.

This meant every cinema had to have a very talented pianist/organist, to convey words and emotion through the medium of music.

If you get a chance to go up Nevill Street towards the pier, you will see a plaque on the wall of 39-41 Nevill Street.

This is the building where George was born.

Following on are two articles containing further information about G.B. Samuelson from the Southport Visiter.

Film Pioneer from Southport

Southport Visiter 20th June 1970

FILM MAGNATE SEES FATHER'S BIRTHPLACE

Film equipment magnate David Samuelson, looked up at the cream building in Nevill St, Southport and recalled a photograph of flags and gaiety taken at the time of Queen Victoria.

It was a picture of a building he knew so well, a tobacconist's, now known as Preston's - the birthplace of his father, Mr. G.B. Samuelson, who became a leading director and pioneer film maker.

And Mr. David Samuelson and his mother were standing outside that very building for the first time in 23 years this week, when they returned to Southport for the "Evening of Silent Cinema."

G.B. Samuelson was educated in Southport and went to school with two of British Theatre's most glamorous leading ladies, Phyllis and Zena Dare.

He got work with a Southport concert party and from then on it was Samuelson the film man. In 1910 he was able, purely by chance, to purchase the newsreel of the funeral of King Edward VII which he rented to a local cinema.

He went to great preparations so that the film of the King's funeral could be shown the same evening. He discovered that there was a train from Paddington to Birkenhead which would arrive by

9:30 p.m. and he arranged with his brother to pick up the film in London, rush it to the station and hand it to the guard of the train. At Birkenhead, a friend was there to meet the train and carry the film by ferry boat to Liverpool where another friend was to take it by motorcycle to Southport - about 20 miles. Nothing like it had ever been attempted before - the showing of a film depicting an event over 200 miles away within a few hours of it happening. "Imagine our dismay when three days before the event an opposition showman announced he would show the film of the funeral."

So dismayed was Samuelson, that he went along to the screening and found the showman had procured a copy of Queen Victoria's funeral!

On July 1, 1914, Samuelson had opened his own studios at Worton Hall, Isleworth, where he began shooting, "A Study In Scarlet." He then returned to Southport for some of the location work and the film's great Mormon Trek was actually filmed on Southport sands.

He later produced innumerable films including "John Halifax Gentlemen"(1915); "The Girl Who Loves A Soldier" (1916); "Dr. Wake's Patient" (1916) "Milestones" (1916) and "The Sorrows Of Satan" (1917). For Mrs. Samuelson and her son David, it was a nostalgic return to a town they both love.

Southport Visiter 26th April 1996

Film pioneer who founded his own dynasty honoured

Southport honoured Bertie Samuelson, a pioneer of silent movies, with a special plaque this week – while his descendents, including Hollywood star, Emma Samms, looked on.

On Wednesday, Bertie's sons, Sidney, David, Anthony and Michael officially unveiled the plaque on Nevill Street to honour the film pioneer, watched by more than 40 members of the Samuelson family, civic dignitaries and councillors.

Bertie Samuelson was born above what was then a tobacconists in Nevill Street in 1889 and started his film career from there in 1910. The Samuelsons were the first Jewish family to settle in Southport.

One of his most famous films was "The Angel of Mons," which told the story of soldiers who reported seeing angels over the lines during the retreat from Mons (Now twinned with Sefton).

He died in 1947, but the Samuelson family were left with cinema in their blood – his four sons are all involved in the industry and grand-daughter, Emma Samms, is famous for her appearances in American soaps "Dynasty" and "The Colbys."

Emma, who returns to Los Angeles for filming duties next week, travelled up to Southport for the unveiling. She never met her illustrious grandfather, but has heard much about him.

She told the Visiter : "There's many members of the family here today that I've never met before.

I have heard so much about my grandfather. I am in awe of him. This is the first time we have been able to do anything to recognise him."

The plaque was put up in association with the British Film Institute as part of this year's "Cinema 100" celebrations marking a centenary of cinema.

Author's note

This is the part of the book which no-one reads. So I'll completely understand if you close the book at this point.

I didn't start writing a book about Hollywood movie stars.

It began with a trip on an open-top bus tour around Southport.

I saw the former Palace Hotel site in Birkdale and began researching this gargantuan icon. Years and years of research took me in many different directions.

Whilst reading lots of old newspapers on microfilm, I would unearth and document, articles about movie stars in Southport. Often the two distinct strands of research would become entangled.

All the Hollywood stories couldn't go in the Palace Hotel book. Another book had to be written.

It has been an absolute pleasure researching the book and it was somewhat deflating when it came to an end.

When I'd found one movie star who had visited Southport, it was like finding treasure. When I discovered several other stars, it became somewhat of an obsession. It also made me wonder whether it could really be true. Hollywood movie stars in Southport? No one will believe me. It seemed too fantastical.

To create an overall picture of each visit by a Hollywood star, I trawled through dozens of biographies, autobiographies, and newspapers while acquiring photographs, postcards and maps of old buildings. I interviewed as many people as was possible, then compiled my findings, like a jigsaw puzzle.

I also had to consider what was relevant and who merited a mention. There are people and places you could argue, should have been included; for example, **Robin Asquith**, an actor born in Southport. He didn't make the cut because he didn't go to Hollywood whereas Miranda Richardson did.

Other notable visitors made only a fleeting visit to Southport and didn't do an interview or particularly take an interest in where they were.

Mickey Rooney, Marlene Dietrich, Diana Dors, Hattie Jacques, Samuel L.Jackson, and **Robbie Coltrane**, would all fall into this category.

The miles of sandy beaches and sand dunes at Ainsdale and Freshfield have been used briefly as a backdrop for several films.

The Rutles (1978) starring Eric Idle, **Hilary and Jackie** (1998) starring Emily Watson, and **Alfie** (2004) starring Jude Law have all used the nearby beach for location filming.

I'm sure this book will bring to light other stories.

Let's hope so anyway.

James Ford

(2009)

Contact information

For all comments, enquiries and requests please email :

enquiries@firestormpublishing.co.uk

enquiries@southportwalkingtours.co.uk

Lightning Source UK Ltd.
Milton Keynes UK
UKOW04f1928190415

249929UK00001B/23/P